Reaching the Top

Factors that Impact the Careers and Retention of Senior Women Leaders

Wanda T. Wallace, Ph.D.

ACKNOWLEDGEMENTS

I would like to thank the women and men who were willing to share their experiences and perspectives. A heartfelt thanks goes to two senior women executives who shared the details of their experiences in the early days of the research project.

A special thank you to the following companies who sponsored the research, helped guide the questions, and listened to early reports on findings:

AstraZeneca   *International Truck and Engine*
British Telecom   *Kellogg*
Cardinal Health   *Motorola*
Deutsche Bank   *PricewaterhouseCoopers*
FleetBoston Financial   *Siemens Financial*
(now Bank of America)

These companies participated along with Brian Hackett in the Women's Leadership Forum.

Lastly, I'm grateful for the support of my colleagues who helped guide the research and the writing: Liam Fahey, Sandy Shullman, and in particular Randy White.

Wanda T. Wallace, Ph.D.
wanda.wallace@leadershipforuminc.com

CONTENTS

Part 1

The Current Status

While significant efforts have been made over the last several years to recruit, develop, and retain talented women, the executive ranks are still dominated by men. According to a 2005 study by Catalyst, Inc., "at the estimated growth trend for the past ten years; it could take 40 years for women to reach parity with men in corporate officer ranks."

For most organizations, the issue is not one of having an adequate number of women in the pipeline. Many have reported recruiting men and women into professional positions at about equal rates for well over the last ten years. However, at some point, the number of women rising in the ranks begins to diminish disproportionately. The drop-off frequently occurs either at or just before the rise to upper management.

For those organizations that have succeeded in getting some women into senior management, there is often a revolving door phenomenon. One woman leaves, another comes in behind her. Thus, the proportion changes very little from year to year. Clearly, it is time for a new perspective on the problem.

Given the dearth of women in leadership positions both in the U.S. and in Europe, this report seeks to address why progress continues at such a slow pace and offers some recommendations for women and their respective employers on what can be done to ensure maximum success for everyone.

According to the 2005 census conducted by the research and advisory company, Catalyst, women represented 16.4% of corporate officers in Fortune 500 companies (up from 15.7% in 2002), a mere 0.7 percentage points.

In a 2006 survey conducted by the Cranfield School of Business with boards of FTSE 100 companies, females held only 10.35% of director positions and only 3.87% of executive director positions, up from 6.4% and 2%, respectively, five years ago. Furthermore, the study reported that women comprise 12.5% of the 181 new board appointments in 2005. This is nearly a 17% reduction from two years prior. Some companies appointed their first-ever women directors, but others reverted to an all-male board. Furthermore, the EU average for women in senior management positions is 10%.

2

THE CURRENT STATUS

With the exception of a few countries, the numbers do not differ greatly around the world. In the U.S., women hold 13.6% of board seats; Canada, 11.2%; Australia, 10.7%; Spain, 4.6%; Japan 0.3%.[1] The U.S. numbers do show improvement with women holding 14.7% of board seats in Fortune 500 companies in 2005, 11.7% in 2000, and 9.6% in 1995.[2] It was not until 2004 that a woman was first named to join the executive board of any of the 30 blue chip companies listed on the German Stock Index.[3] Furthermore, only 11% of German companies have a woman in a management positions (the EU average is 14%).[4]

The executive search firm, Korn Ferry International, in collaboration with the Columbia Business School and the Duran Group, conducted a study of 425 women who left the corporate ranks to join entrepreneurial companies as owners or as workers.[5] These women left jobs as vice presidents,

[1] Corporate Women Directors International, www.globewomen.com/cwdi/cwdi.asp, cited July 9, 2004.

[2] 2005 Catalyst Census of Women Corporate Officers and Top Earners, www.catalystwomen.org. cited August 13, 2006.

[3] "For German Women, Glass Ceiling Hands Low," *Deutsche Welle*, July 7, 2004, (http://www.dw-world.de/english/0,3367,1431_A_1263544,00.html) cited August 14, 2004.

[4] Ibid.

[5] "What Women Want in Business: A Survey of Executives and Entrepreneurs," Korn Ferry International, 2001.

directors and managers primarily to pursue new opportunities that gave them a chance to take risks with new ideas, impact strategic issues, and create wealth. In addition, these women reported that 1) more time with family and friends (51%), 2) less organizational politicking (48%), and 3) lack of recognition for work (43%) were also contributing factors in their departure from the corporate world.

The C200 Business Leadership Index assesses the clout women hold in business relative to men. A score of 10 would indicate parity with men. In the 2005 index, women reached a score of 5.06 out of 10, an increase of 9% over 2004.[6]

When it comes to line positions, the percentage of female leaders is even more disturbing. According to a study by Catalyst in 2005, only 10.6% of corporate line positions were held by women (up 0.78 percentage points from 2002).[7] As we will see later in this report, holding a line position is an important factor in establishing credibility.

Catalyst also reported that 6.4% of top earners in Fortune 500 companies were women, up 1.2% in 2002.

---

[6] The C200 Business Leadership Index 2005: Annual Report on Women's Clout in Business, The Committee of 200.

[7] *2005 Catalyst Census of Women Corporate Officers and Top Earners* of the *Fortune 500* www.catalystwomen.org, cited August 13, 2006.

THE CURRENT STATUS

If this is the state of affairs and with the expectation of parity between men and women, our research goal was to examine the factors that lead to this disparity.

Part 2

Research Study

Methodology

In-depth interviews were conducted with 64 senior women who were identified by member companies or who were identified through other sources. The interviews were conducted as a guided conversation on the personal experience of each woman.

Profile of Women Interviewed

- 53 women were currently in an organization and were either a part of the executive team, a direct report of a member of the executive team, or top talent not more than four levels beneath the CEO. The representative organizations were all large global companies, either listed in *Fortune's* 500, *Financial Times'* 500, or *Fortune's Global* 500). Organizations were headquartered in the U.S., U.K. or Germany.

- 11 women had left the large corporate world. These women met the same criteria as listed above. In their last large corporate positions they were either part of the executive team, a direct report of a member of the executive team, or top talent not more than four levels beneath the CEO.

- Ages ranged from 32 to 58, with an average age of 46. Age distribution is as follows:

35 or under	3 (5%)
36 to 40	5 (8%)
41 to 45	16 (25%)
46 to 50	18 (28%)
Over 51	12 (19%)
Age unknown	10 (15%)

- Most were married (84% or 47 out of the 56 who provided their marital status).
- Most had children still at home (53% or 30 of 57 for whom the data is available). Others had children who were not living at home (11% or 6 of 57 for whom data is available). Some 37% (21 out of 57) did not have children. These numbers are consistent with other studies of women in senior ranks (Hewlett reported more than a third of women in senior positions in the U.S. do not have children).[8]
- Of the women who were married and had children at home, only 5 spouses were in traditional corporate positions. The remaining 21 spouses in families with

---

[8] S.A. Hewlett, "Executive Women and the Myth of Having it All," *Harvard Business Review,* April 2002, pg 66-73.

children at home were either unemployed, self-employed, worked from home, or worked in jobs that had flexible schedules. For 15 people, some portion of the data is unknown. Across the entire sample, regardless of whether there were children at home or not, a total of 9 (22%) out of 41 husbands for whom data is known are in corporate positions.

- 25 of the women were in general management roles (i.e., roles with customer contact, P&L responsibility, or an operational responsibility) and 36 of the women were in a functional role. 3 were unknown. However, if we exclude those in consulting industries, the number in general management drops to 20. This is compareable to the percentage reported in *Breaking the Glass Ceiling*[9] where 63% of the 76 women interviewed were in functional roles.

Profile of Men Interviewed

In addition, 26 in-depth interviews were conducted with male colleagues or the bosses of these 64 women. The purpose of those interviews was to understand the male perspective on what they believed did and did not contribute to the women's leadership effectiveness.

---

[9] A. Morrison, R. White, E. Van Velsor, *Breaking the Glass Ceiling,* 1987, 1991.

Research Focus and Issues

The focus of this research centers on why women are choosing to leave the corporate world, the role of the corporate experience in fostering that exodus, what organizations can do to retain this talent, and what women can do to increase their effectiveness. The intent is to understand what encourages women to stay with the corporation and what brings them to look for other alternatives. Such insights will help increase the length of time that senior women remain with a corporation, the effectiveness of senior women, the number of senior women in the corporation, and the career development opportunities for women who choose to enter the senior ranks.

The issues within this study could just as easily be asked of any number of other groups within the corporation including ethnic minorities, minority nationalities (e.g., Japanese in a U.S. firm or vice versa), anyone holding a unique competency in a culture dominated by another competency (e.g., marketing orientation in an engineering oriented firm) and of men in general. Many of the issues are not necessarily unique to women or to feminine characteristics. Given the limited number of women in senior positions in large western organizations and the impact if they leave, it is important to understand the career dynamics for at least this one group.

RESEARCH STUDY

Perhaps understanding senior women's experiences can shed light on the challenges for other minority voices.

The key research questions were as follows:

- What experiences were women having in senior positions?
- Why are women considering leaving the corporate ranks?
- What contributes to the success and effectiveness of senior women?
- What can women and corporations do to retain critical talent?

Part 3

The Corporate Experience of the Women Interviewed

Family pressures, work/life balance issues, and ambitions are individual choices that affect both men and women. Individuals of either gender choose to draw those balances to suit themselves. None of these explains why senior women who have already made these choices and who are clearly ambitious are now choosing to exit the corporate world. Rather than focusing on the individual choice factors, we will look at the experiences of women in the senior ranks as one element in understanding the exodus. The purposes here are to understand what organizations can do differently to retain and even increase the number of senior women *and* to understand what women can do to improve their own effectiveness, sense of satisfaction, and opportunities for continued learning.

Five Factors that Impact the Careers and Retention of Senior Women

There is no common experience for all 64 women as individuals because they differ markedly from each other in how they experience the corporate world and in how they interpret that experience. However, in examining the experiences across women in the senior ranks, some distinct patterns emerge. These patterns are interconnected – as one pattern emerges it can compound the effects of another pattern, a problem in one pattern can result in problems in another pattern. No single pattern seems to result in the questioning of career choices; however, when two or three of them occur at the same time, questions about the value of staying in the corporate world typically begin to surface.

- **The Breadth and Quality of Relationships at Work**
  Women in senior positions often do not have as many strong peer-to-peer relationships as their most successful male counterparts. This means that women are less connected to emerging opportunities, have fewer sources of informal information, and have a harder time getting properly recognized and making their contributions known to their organizations.

- **Centrality of the Boss**
  The relationships between women and their superiors are often less than ideal. First, women generally do not receive the type of mentoring and advocacy that successful men receive. Second, women tend to rely too heavily on a single boss for career support; or when women find themselves with a new boss whom they had not known before, the relationship is tent-

ative and fragile. Third, women are not getting concrete, informal feedback on performance and leadership.

- **Sources of Credibility:**
  What Efforts are Perceived as Valued

  Women tend to gain much of their credibility based on performance and expertise. This can keep women so narrowly focused on the job and on their specific skills that they miss strategic business opportunities. In addition, they often do not ask for or are not considered for broader opportunities. Finally, without sufficient breadth of experience across the organization, women are not seen as "credible" leaders by the organization.

- **Genuineness, Accessibility, Predictability and Authenticity**

  Peers and superiors often perceive women as lacking confidence, unable to relax and be themselves, difficult to get to know, and uncomfortable in their roles or with their authority. Whether or not these attributions are fairly portrayed, they can keep women from the opportunities they seek.

- **Perceived Sense of Isolation**

  Women feel isolated in many ways, whether it is perceived or real. When one feels isolated, the inevitable setbacks and challenges in senior roles are difficult to acknowledge as not being personal, advice becomes harder to find, and a balanced perspective can be a challenge to maintain.

Examples

A younger woman, whom the organization saw as part of the next generation of emerging talent and a person with tremendous potential, was moved into a staff position. She found that while she had been very successful in her former role, she was now struggling in the new role. In the old role, rather than having to work through the network of people around her, she had presented the rational argument for a course of action, and if that was not persuasive, she would use her boss' authority to get agreement on an action. Now, in the staff role, she could no longer rely on the boss' power and authority; rather, she had to persuade people, and work with and through many more people and many more layers in the organization to get things done.

Another woman, in a senior functional role with tremendous responsibility to deliver critical assets for the organization, noted that her peers respected her knowledge of her function and they would seek her opinion when the functional area was critical. However, they did not engage her in strategic business discussions around issues such as re-organization. Furthermore, she noted the sense of isolation she felt when her peers came to meetings together, and she came and left alone.

(Examples Cont.)

A third woman failed to receive a promotion she sought and felt she was highly qualified for. The man who received the position was, in her opinion, less experienced and less qualified. When she asked why she had not received the promotion, the feedback was nebulous and inactionable – she was told she was not ready and was not strategic enough. At this point, many women would have left the corporation – she was talented, successful, and in high demand. However, the woman chose to become a student of what the men around her were doing. She found that when there was a rumor of a re-organization or acquisition, the men were in and out of the boss' office daily, talking about possible new structures, new ways of framing the business, and other potential actions given the opportunity presented by the re-organization or acquisition. Due to these regular conversations, the boss knew how the men thought about the business, knew they were ambitious, and knew what they would probably do if given the opportunity. Because the woman stayed in her office getting her job done, rather than "wasting" time chatting, no one was aware of what she thought about, cared about or what opportunities interested her.

These five factors as shown in Figure 1 below interact. For example, relying on expertise as a base of credibility and authority can reinforce the lack of operational exposure. The problem is that a woman may be more comfortable in her current functional role and less willing to seek an operational role which in turn can limit her exposure to peers in other parts of the organization. Another example is that depending upon the boss, not having operational experience to broaden exposure along with not having sufficiently strong peer networks can reinforce the need to seek approval. This results in an even further sense of isolation as peers interpret efforts to seek approval as a lack of confidence.

Figure 1
Five Interactive Factors that Impact the Careers and Retention of Senior Women Leaders

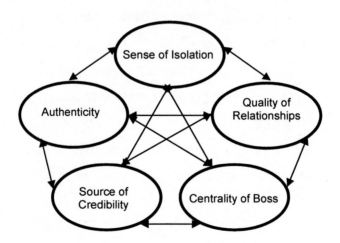

In the next section, each of the five patterns will be examined separately.

The Breadth and Quality of Relationships at Work

Senior leadership (top four levels including the CEO) in most organizations can be distinguished by the following characteristics:

- Nothing can be accomplished alone. Collaboration from other groups is needed, as well as cross-group expertise and/or cross-group information and resources.
- The perspective is more that of the corporation rather than that of a single line of business.
- Almost all decisions have a shade of grey and a high level of uncertainty about the best possible course of action.
- The decisions involve multi-faceted, complex issues.

As one definition of leadership states: Leadership is finding the solution that will be accepted by the greatest number of people in the least amount of time and leads to the greatest competitive advantage.[10]

In that type of environment, the quality of peer-to-peer relationships is critical. That is, to be effective, senior leaders

[10] P. Hodgson and R. White, *Relax! It's Only Uncertainty,* Financial Times, 2001.

need to, at minimum, know how the other thinks, be able to get information from different groups quickly, be able to influence others to join the recommended course of action, and be able to call in favors. As one male leader put it (describing a woman in his organization whom he thought was extremely talented, but whom he would not promote): "You are only a leader if your peers are willing to follow you. Her peers are not willing to follow her." In his view, she had great talent in her current role, but could not assume more responsibility without the support of her peers.

There are several things that are currently working against women developing the quality of relationships that are necessary to function effectively at the top of the organization. Among these are the breadth of different relationships women hold across the corporation, the participation in informal strategic discussions particularly during periods of change, the pattern of promotions for women, and the opportunities for informal, social interaction. Here, women, men and the organization can all take some actions that can improve the situation.

Breadth of Relationships

Women report spending relatively little time interacting informally with male colleagues – not that they are not capable of networking, rather that they choose to spend their time differently. According to Joyce K. Fletcher, women are

20

more task and results oriented than their male counterparts. In her study, she observes, "Women scored higher on leadership scales measuring an orientation toward setting high standards of performance and the attainment of results."[11] Thus, a common report is as follows: A woman, aware that she has to perform or over-perform to keep her position focuses on getting the job done. She focuses on building her team and spending time with her team. In addition, because she wants to get home to family (or friends outside work), she knows that she has to skip chit-chat or lunch in order to get the job done.

Women view relationships outside of the immediate tasks as tactical, transactional, respectful, and friendly. What they do not see is the broader range of relationships that can be strategically advantageous. Note that when women work closely with others (e.g., team, boss, cross-unit, or peers); they then tend to build strong relationships. The difference, and a paradox for talented women interested in delivering superb performance, is that women do not see the time spent on informal relationships as useful in performing the current job, as an investment in future job performance, and as a strategic necessity.

---

[11] Joyce K. Fletcher, *Disappearing Acts: Gender, Power, and Relational Practice at Work*, MIT Press, 1999.

> **One woman described her choices the following way:**
> The only way I can maintain any sort of balance is to leave work by 6 p.m. to get home to my family. By doing so, I think I am setting a positive example for other women in the organization. However, in order to get my job done I have to be very focused on the task and be very judicious with my time. I don't spend time talking with people unless there is something urgent we have to discuss about the work at hand.

In the example above, the woman is focusing on the *relationship* – the one(s) that is (are) critical for that task at that moment in time – rather than focusing on building *relationships* broadly and generally for current and future positions. When women choose the former pattern of behavior they are missing several important components. One, only the men who have worked directly with them on tasks know anything about what they do or how they think. Two, they do not know enough people in the organization to get information when they need it and they do not know much about what will persuade others to agree to a recommendation. Many have noted the ability to persuade a broad range of people to follow one's recommendations as a key feature of a general manager's job.[12] Three, they develop little sense of easy camaraderie with their peers.

---

[12] e.g., R. Kelly, *The Power of Followership,* Doubleday, 1992.; J. Kotter, *General Managers,* Free Press, 1982.

In describing the strategy of focusing on work and avoiding talking with people unless necessary to the task, one man had the following reaction: "That will never work. In order to get *anything* done I probably touch at least a hundred people. I could not reach that many people if I did not drop by offices to touch base, chat with people in the hall, catch people at the elevator. I simply could not accomplish my goals without the ability to call in favors, to pick up the phone and ask someone I chat with to get information to me."

Men routinely describe the necessity of having interactions with people that are not just about work. They report that one has to talk about something other than work – people need to have a sense of who you are which they cannot get from conversations about work alone.

As one senior man describes: "I can learn more about a person in a 5 minute discussion about something he/she is passionate about than I can in an hour discussion about his/her strategy."

Women generally tend to believe that you have to have a business issue to discuss with someone in order to start a conversation, whereas men report an interest in building common ground on something of mutual interest before they discuss a business issue. As most of the men say, the common ground is what makes the job fun – the job is tough enough, you have to have some fun. Interestingly, one of the reasons women are leaving the corporate world is they are not having enough fun. Part of the challenge and frustration for women in the corporate world is discovering the common ground with their colleagues.

The men who were interviewed were very clear that sports talk was not the only or the best way to create common ground. In fact, many of them reported not liking the sports talk themselves. They were all in agreement, though, with the need to have something to talk about other than work. They believed women could choose any topic they wanted just as long as it was one of mutual interest.

Some examples:

One man commented on a woman who was very effective in client relationships when either the client or the client's spouse had an interest in the arts.

One man remarked on talking about family as a sense of common ground. However, he noted that talking about the tension of being away from the family was not a good idea. A child's achievement – sports or otherwise – was probably more likely to create common ground.

One man talked about trying to build a critical relationship with a very senior, very distant leader. He sought a point of common ground and found it in his children's nationality and heritage through their mother's side. Taking the time to find the common ground and build interactions based on it proved invaluable in creating a relationship with this executive.

Men in client-serving businesses were very clear that women would not be able to hold senior level positions unless they could build relationships with clients. In their opinion, the relationship was far more important than the quality of the financial recommendation. Many people could give quality recommendations. What distinguished successful client engagements was the quality of the relationship and the common perspective built outside of the business discussion itself.

So long as one's position is not at the very senior ranks or remains within a functional area, the narrower set of peers is probably fine. As soon as an individual needs to influence across areas, the breadth of relationships becomes a critical factor in success. The women who have developed a broad set of peer relationships within the corporation stand out as far more effective, far more respected, and far more satisfied with corporate life.

An example of the importance of strong peer relationships: One woman who had a broad, strong peer network because of the number of different businesses in which she had worked, received a call from a peer with a warning about an effort a more senior executive was making to establish unethical behavior on her part. Because of the call, she had time to collect the appropriate data to document her own position, largely without the senior executive's knowledge. When the case was eventually mentioned, she had all the information she needed to defend herself in a calm, collected manner. She came across as an effective leader. The other executive left the company shortly thereafter.

Another example: One man commented on the frequency with which a male subordinate dropped by his office – either to mention an accomplishment or to ask his advice or opinion. His remark was that both were very effective in building knowledge about the subordinate and in establishing a relationship. He noted with surprise that no female subordinates had ever asked his opinion. He thought they were missing an opportunity to build a relationship. Other men made similar remarks.

In summary, the peer network is not as broad or extensive for some women as for successful senior men. If women examine their social networks within the organization in comparison to men they believe are in stronger positions than they are, then they will likely find that both women and men have networks, but that the extent of the network will be much broader for men and perhaps include more of the key opinion leaders in the organization.

Informal Discussions in Times of Change

When corporations are going through a merger or a re-organization, several women noted the pattern of conversation among men. They noted that the men spent a great deal of time talking with each other about the implications – speculating about possible structures, going into the boss every other day with a new idea on how to re-structure, exchanging thoughts on how to run a piece of the business differently, and so forth. The women were amazed at how the men had so much time to chat about the situation. They also felt that much of the effort was "buttering-up" the boss or gossiping. However, in the end, many noted that a number of these men ended up in significant roles. While the women were sitting in their offices focusing on the tasks to be done, the men were engaged in strategic discussions about possibilities. As a result, bosses knew at least two things about the men: one is that they aspired to a larger role, and the other is how they thought about the business. This same insight was not necessarily afforded to the women who sat in their offices.

Cycle of Promotions for Women

The following story was reported often: The CEO becomes concerned about the lack of senior women – usually because clients are asking about diversity initiatives, customers are becoming more diverse, there is a concern about the scarcity of talent, or daughters are entering the corporate workforce. He rallies the senior leadership team to find and promote more women. With the best of intent, senior executives look into their ranks, identify a talented woman and promote her, typically one or two steps faster than she would normally have been promoted. Not a bad outcome until one examines the net effect on that woman:

In one case, a woman was promoted two or three steps ahead of her current peer group, stayed in that position for longer than the peer group, and then was promoted ahead again. She felt like her career was a ping-pong ball, subject to the whims of the current hot topic. Her male peers did not develop a stable relationship with her as at one moment she was ahead of them, at the next they were ahead of her.

In another example, a woman so promoted had three strikes against her. First, she did not really have quite enough experience to do the job in which she was suddenly placed. Corporations do this to men all the time, yet they expect male bosses, peers, and some subordinates to provide support while the person learns. However, in this case, the woman's peers resented the fact that she was suddenly above them when they had worked hard to get to their current positions. In that climate, they were more willing to sit back and watch her handle the job because "if she is so good then she should be able to work it out." Perhaps the woman also felt she had a lot to prove and was reluctant to seek help. Either way, she was on her own in a job for which she was not adequately prepared. Not only was this a huge job, but to make matters worse, she was now the only woman at a senior level, she was expected to be on every committee, to chair the women's network, to attend four times as many client events, and be a mentor to more women than a human being could possibly manage. In her case, it was a no-win situation with a less-than-positive outcome for everyone. Needless to say, she failed.

A few men noted experiences where a woman was not promoted because a male colleague had been very ambitious and because the organization felt he would likely leave if he did not receive the promotion, whereas they felt the woman would wait for another opportunity.

Women were asked about their cycles of promotion and whether they thought they were promoted faster than male peers, at about the same pace or slower. The response was mixed. Many felt they were at pace or faster early on in their career. Some believed they were promoted at a slower pace starting at mid-career. However, many had been in the current assignment for three or four years. Needless to say, as "fast trackers" throughout most of their careers, they were getting restless and were often looking to leave, especially when the average fast track executive moves about every 18 to 24 months. As already noted, since the new opportunities are one of the keys to retaining senior women, organizations should question whether or not they are keeping women in roles longer than male peers at comparable levels. If so, the practice probably contributes to high exit rates among women.

Social Interactions

Women and men acknowledged that the opportunities for social interactions have been reduced as organizations have cut back on sales meetings, annual meetings, and special

31

events. When the women were asked about their level of social interaction with peers, most felt there was very little. A few would go out for a drink after work, though most would prefer not to do so. Very few reported going out to dinner with peers. Many cited the challenges of getting together for lunch. Many women did not take a break for lunch preferring to continue work. Several women commented on rarely being included in lunch invitations noting that men usually went together. Several women commented that even if they invited a male colleague to lunch, the invitation was never reciprocated. Many women noted that the social interaction among some male peers included getting families together over the weekend, playing golf together on the weekend, having kids on the same soccer team, or having wives who were close friends. None of the women reported having such relationships with their male peers. In addition, the spouses of the women were put into an awkward situation. When they needed to interact at a corporate function, were they supposed to gravitate toward other spouses (females) or toward their wife's peers (males)? For many spouses of women the social interaction was not easy – did they talk with other spouses or discuss business with the men?

In fairness, many of the men who were interviewed also reported that they had relatively little social interaction with peers, especially with families. Although, many did report going to lunch or for a drink or a meal after work. Several felt this time for informal discussion was critical for building a sense of camaraderie, developing the relationship, and creating common ground. Many of the men noted that when women were pulled home to be with the kids, they missed the type of interaction that occurred after work or over dinner.

Creating any opportunity, however, to interact with men in any social setting is not necessarily a good idea as the following story illustrates:

As one man reported: I love to play golf. The guys know that and of course they try to find opportunities to play with me. However, for a woman to take up golf just to play with the guys is not smart. The other month a woman joined up for a round. But she didn't love the game and she wasn't very good. I can tell you it did not help her. I love excellence. I want to see passion. You have to find something that you are good at and that you love as a basis to interact. It can be about anything – it doesn't have to be golf just because I like golf.

It is impossible to tell whether the lack of social interaction outside of work occurs because men and women are uncomfortable in the available settings (e.g., drinks or dinner), because men and women have relatively little common interests, because women feel the need to be home with family, or for other unspoken reasons. Whether organizations are comfortable with the discussion or not, a tension exists between men and women being friends and peers versus having a more intimate relationship either in reality or as interpreted by peers or spouses.[13]

---

[13] This is not an easy or popular topic and certainly one I never expected to mention. However, as I conducted the interviews I was overwhelmed by the number of times that women began describing an unwelcome sexual advance that they did not know how to handle. At senior levels, there were even 6 stories out of 64 which shocked me, many more acknowledged encountering this earlier in their careers. A surprising number were boss to subordinates. I tackle this topic because I believe it is one we must learn to discuss. I think the issue is not how to prevent any and all sexual advances in the workplace. I presume all women at this level have a clear sense of themselves and what they believe sends the wrong signals within their corporate environment. I do not want to advise what is or is not appropriate – this is up to individual judgment.

Rather, I think we need to acknowledge that sexual advances do occur and discuss strategies for managing those in ways that do not damage the relationship. Let me give an observation that illustrates the reason for this statement. In 4 out of the 6 stories I heard, the women did not broach the subject of a relationship issue until the man made an overt gesture – subtle or otherwise. For these 4, they hoped that if they did not say anything, the problem would disappear. When they finally did approach the topic, the response to the man was strong and definitive. In all 4 cases, relationships were damaged in ways that made it difficult to work together. We have to ask whether or not early acknowledgement, a sense of humor, a gentle rejection or some other tactic would have left the relationship less damaged. For example, one of the 6 stories had a positive outcome and did not damage the relationship. The woman simply used humor early to acknowledge the extra attention and to note that if she had met him before her husband then she might have been interested, but not now. They remained colleagues and friends.

In summary, the quality of peer relationships is a key factor in success. For relationships to be strategically advantageeous, women need to think of them as such, build broad relationships with people across the organization, spend more time in discussions with peers, and find more common ground with male peers. To the extent that women are seen by male peers as equal in terms of the ease of interaction, men tend to evaluate women as having great leadership potential.

Centrality of the Boss

The relationship between women and their boss is critical and was often less than ideal. First, many women in this study tended to rely heavily on a single boss for feedback, recognition, and the identification of career opportunities. Second, women generally did not receive the type of mentoring (e.g., "godfathering") that successful men received. Third, when most women found themselves with a new boss whom they had not known before, they found the relationship to be difficult and lacking ease as they struggled to get to know the boss, to build a deeper relationship, and to establish mutual trust.

I do not think there are any clear answers. I do think we need to acknowledge the potentials and talk about effective strategies that would have lessened the damage to the relationship.

Getting Feedback

Most senior executives report not getting good feedback on behavior – executives tend to know what has or has not been done (i.e., performance), but not how well it was done (i.e., behavior). In fact, in leadership seminars, one of the things participants most value is getting qualitative feedback about how they are doing and what they can improve in their leadership effectiveness. For women, the situation is confused – they need feedback as leaders, they seem to want more support and feedback than male colleagues, but men fear providing feedback because of either the emotional reactions or the potential for legal action.

Several women in this study found themselves seeking a new position and getting turned down. When asked why, the feedback was always ambiguous – nothing concrete, nothing to work on, nothing to develop. They were enormously frustrated. At this point, if they could see something to improve they tended to stay with the organization and be challenged by learning. If they could not see how or what to improve, they tended to consider leaving the organization. When women do not see many women succeeding at the top, if they do not get feedback that helps them improve, and if they are turned down for a position, then they tend to conclude that the organization does not support women or that there is no opportunity for women at the top. The lack of clear feedback is likely the same for men as it is for

36

women; however, the sense of opportunities for men is very different and the conclusions drawn about the lack of feedback can also be very different.

Several men also noted, quite openly, that they were confused about the best way to handle the situation for fear of being sued, or because they were afraid a woman would cry and they would not know how handle the situation. Some admitted that they avoided giving negative, even constructive feedback, as a result of these concerns.

Example

One woman noted that if her female colleagues received better feedback, they could manage the situation better. In her case, she found that if she approached a male peer one-on-one and asked him directly what she could have done better in a presentation; then, she would get very good input. The key was to ask directly for constructive feedback on the assumption that every presentation could be improved. The second key was to ask one-on-one, never in a group.

In terms of advice for men in managing tears, one woman described the following approach from her boss: He would bring her into his office to give her feedback. He would let her rant and rave, cry, and hand her a box of tissues until she got the emotion out. Then, they would discuss strategies. According to her, this was fairly quick and exactly what she needed. Several women commented that men should just not worry if there are tears – so what!

Recognition and Promotion

For most of the women in the study, promotions and new opportunities came when a boss recognized performance or when a boss (current or former) told them to consider a particular position that was open. With very few exceptions, women do not report actively seeking the next position. Instead, most report typically waiting for someone to ask them.

Women do note, often with distaste, watching male colleagues "jockey" for the next position. As one woman described, "I have watched male peers and subordinates. From the moment many of them take a position, they are working to get the next one by positioning themselves, lobbying and looking for an opportunity."

Men, when asked what advice they would give to their daughters about working in the corporate world, almost unilaterally gave at least the following advice: 1) Be clear about what you want in your career and be aggressive about getting yourself into a position to achieve those goals, 2) Be direct with superiors about your goals and ambitions, and 3) Manage your career carefully.

One man described the situation this way: "Women have the right to demand to know more about opportunities for their careers... they are not doing it." **Another man said,** "Yes, the men who succeed are far more likely to drop by my door in the evening to tell me that they just had a great call with a client. Women tend to wait until something big has happened rather than giving me regular updates... I call the men the door hangers. Yes, I know that these men are just promoting themselves – but give me credit for being able to distinguish between what is real and what is BS. However, I have to also admit that the squeaky wheel usually gets the most attention."

Another stated: One of my most important jobs is assigning bonuses. I spend a lot of time each year trying to get this right – it matters a great deal to people and I try to consider all the information I have about each person. In truth, the more I know about a person, the more likely I am to get it right. When men tell me about their aspirations and goals, I have more information to get it right. Women should do more of this.

Women admit that they do not go by a boss' office to regularly report small successes. Rather, they prefer to wait until a larger goal is accomplished and report the performance results of that goal. Women also acknowledge that they do not tend to ask advice, preferring instead to show that they can do the job.

Mentors and Sponsors

The most successful executives typically have a senior level sponsor who takes them under his (or her) wing early in the career, advises them on how to navigate the corporate politics, gives them candid feedback on presentations/performance, advocates that they have assignments on key task forces-projects, engages them in high level strategic debate when they are in junior positions, makes sure they are have the right connections in the organization, or at least some subset of these.

An example: One man described his most significant mentor this way: "I guess he saw me sort of like a son. He would advise me on how to present an argument. He made sure I had certain experiences. More importantly, he needed someone to talk with. So when he was struggling with a strategic issue he would bring me into his office and quiz me about what he should do in a particular case. I'd give an answer and he'd say 'no that won't work because...' Over the years with debates like that I learned a lot more than I thought. In fact, I didn't know how much I had learned until I took this new (more senior) position."

The type of relationship and guidance described in the above example goes well beyond the typical mentoring relationship. It is almost a godfather relationship. Most of the men interviewed had a relationship like this early in their careers

– some had more than one. This type of relationship is a central theme for many men.[14]

When women were asked about mentors in their careers, many, though not all, reported having a mentor. However, the descriptions of the relationship are very different than the one described. For the most part, the women reported having a boss who had been impressed with their performance. That boss did things such as review a presentation with them, gave advice or encouraged them to apply for a particular position. Sometimes when the boss took a new role, the woman would follow and also receive a promotion; which proved to be rewarding and helpful to their careers. On the other hand, when the boss left the company, careers would sometimes stagnate. Overall however, these detached relationships are not of the same quality as the "godfather" one noted above.

---

[14] D. Levinson, *Seasons of a Man's Life,* 1978.

Another story to illustrate the point: A man was describing a talented woman in his organization. He was asked about her mentor and named someone he thought was probably mentoring ("godfathering") her. Then he was asked to describe the three most important junior people for this mentor – the three people this mentor would watch out for, advocate for promotions, and protect. Quickly, the interviewee rattled off three names without thinking. The woman was not among that set. That is the difference between mentoring by offering advice and "godfathering" by advocating, protecting, molding, and guiding.

To a great extent, women are not receiving the same guidance, training, or assistance as the very select, but fortunate men. Executives usually take on such "godfathering" roles with someone they like, whom they can relate to, and who reminds them of themselves. To the degree that senior executives are mostly men, the implication is that mostly younger men will continue to be selected. However, expecting the few senior women to take on these roles is asking too much. One, they are already over-extended in corporate citizenship because there are so few women. Two, the need is too high for only one or two women to make a sufficient difference. Three, some women do not want to be seen as only mentoring/sponsoring women. Four, the women may not be sufficiently connected within the organization to be a good "godmother."

There is a second, more significant problem for women around the mentoring issue. In most of the cases, the mentors who women named were bosses. They described that boss as important to them because he suggested a new assignment, encouraged them to go for a promotion, etc. For many, this was the only "role model" relationship they had in the organization. Thus, the boss takes on a far too central role. Research on the primary reasons leaders derail and are either asked to leave or are sidelined points to an overdependence on a boss or other mentor who later leaves or falls out of favor in the organization.[15]

The Quality of the Relationship with the Boss

Some women had an experience with one boss who was very supportive over an extended period of time. On the other hand, many women in the sample, when asked about the quality of the relationship with the current boss, knew this relationship was not what it should be, especially if they were relatively new to this boss. For some, the relationship had been filled with tension since he took the role. For only a few was the relationship strong.

---

[15] M. McCall and M. Lombardo, "What Makes a Top Executive?" *Psychology Today, 17* (2), pg 26-31, 1983.

The following story was conveyed several times: A new boss had been in the role for about a year or a bit less. The woman and this boss had never really worked together on a project or in another position. She did not know how to relate to him or did not know what he really wanted. There was no feedback either way from the boss. So, her strategy was to focus on her job and deliver the results. At about the year mark, though, rumors started to emerge through peers or even subordinates that the boss did not think she had done a presentation or other interaction particularly well. The boss continued to complain to others. She did not focus on improving the relationship until it was largely irreparable. By this point, the boss had decided that she needed to move on – either because he had someone else to put in the role that he knew from a former position, he wanted to re-organize her area, or he had mounted a case that she was not a strong leader. Typically, at this point, the woman's confide-ence in her leadership capability was diminished and/or her confidence in the organizational support for women in general was diminished. With a decline in confidence, her credibility was damaged. The same scenario probably happ-ens with men as well. Those men also end up not being effective.

In summary, if women are not building strong relationships with bosses, getting support from a boss, being mentored, gaining attention through appropriate self-promotion, being overly dependent on a boss or actively seeking new growth opportunities and new assignments, then they are not likely to be promoted. If the challenge is to increase the effectiveness and number of women in the senior positions, then the organization cannot afford to continue to lose potential talent without intervening earlier in the process. Both the organization and the women have responsibility to intervene or to seek help early enough to make a difference.

Sources of Credibility: What Efforts are Perceived as Valued

In all organizations, leaders develop credibility over the course of their careers. Leaders' credibility comes as a result of what they have achieved for the organization, how they manage through tough times, how they accomplish goals, who is willing to follow them, and even the confidence or presence they convey. In this section, the ways in which women approach issues that build credibility are considered: performance, teams and followers, confidence and presence.

Performance: Meeting Targets, Area of Expertise, Meritocractic Cultures

Overwhelmingly, women believe that they have to outperform their male colleagues to get the same gains and opportunities. They estimate that they have to work anywhere from 120% to 200% as much. Many of their male peers agree. Women believe that if they do not perform, they will be out. For the women in this study, performance never seems to have been the issue. They report over and over again about delivering numbers above expectations. There seems to be sense of pride in the ability to repeatedly deliver more than was expected.

In this climate of over-performance, it is possible that women are more perfectionistic than their equally successful male peers. Women regularly talked about competing with themselves (as individuals) to do more than they thought they could do and to deliver above and beyond the expectations. They also recognized that sometimes male peers were quite comfortable doing the minimum necessary. It is unclear whether or not women are truly over-performing; whether this is an advantage to their careers or not; whether this keeps them too narrowly focused to advance or not; whether or not they are more hesitant to take stretch assignments because they fear the drop in performance that results from a major change; whether or not they are less likely to seek peer help; and whether or not time could be better utilized in broader peer interactions. Any tendency towards over-performing, whether justified or not, is likely to be compounded by a sense of isolation.

An Example: In one interview, a woman described a very difficult time for the organization. "I had an impossible job that was unrealistic for anyone. I had the challenge of downsizing a part of the organization which required huge cuts in the workforce. I met the target, but with great agony to the organization – and I regret what I did to people – good people who were valuable contributors to the organization and whom the organization truly needed as we came out of that crisis. Those cuts were not a good long-term strategy for the organization. I should have talked more to my colleagues – the men also thought the goals were unreasonable and they simply chose not to deliver those goals. They were not worried about turning in the exact numbers and nothing happened when they did not achieve their targets. I was the only one who did. I wish I had done what they did. I believed at that time that I had to deliver the results." The question is whether she did have to deliver or whether she was holding herself to an unrealistic standard. And clearly, had she been less isolated, she might have seen other options.

If performance is over-emphasized by women, then they should thrive in organizations that look more closely at performance. Women report believing the corporation should be a meritocracy where people are promoted based on performance and experience, not on connections or favoritism. When women find that the best performers are not the ones being promoted, they tend to want to leave the organization.

Catalyst (2004) reported that organizations with more women in senior level positions have better financial performance. The study concluded that promoting women to senior positions was the cause of this improved performance. The reverse may also be true – organizations with strong financial performance tend to promote women. Here is the logic: Organizations with strong financial performance tend to be in growth mode; there are many opportunities; so, these organizations are willing to take more risks by promoting people who are different from the norm, including women. However, when these organizations have to tighten controls and there are fewer opportunities, as when financial performance begins to decline, women are not as likely to get as many opportunities and are likely to lose gains that they have made. When organizations are less willing to take risks, any leader who is different will be considered an added risk that the organization may avoid.

Finally, most women rise through the ranks in one functional area. Thus, they have relatively little cross-unit exposure and therefore have worked with fewer people in the organization. Not many people truly know these women, know how they think, or know why they should listen to their opinions. We have recognized for years that effective general managers transition through various businesses as they develop their career.[16]

On this issue, not much has changed in 25 years. According to a recent Center for Creative Leadership study, women were not given international, operational and P&L assignments.[17]

The women in this study are no exception. By and large, they are in functional roles – heads of HR, marketing, R&D, CFO, CIO, chief legal counsel, or the like – positions that have been called "the velvet ghetto". Very rarely are they in operational roles such as manufacturing or with significant P&L assignments (only 7 out of 64). Those who aspire to a line or operational role find that they cannot move.

---

[16] e.g., M. McCall, M. Lombardo, and A. Morrison, *Lessons of Experience*, 1988.

[17] M. Ruderman & P. Ohlot, *Standing at the Crossroads: Next Steps for High-Achieving Women*, 2002.

Two examples: A very successful senior woman was unhappy and distressed about her inability to get out of a functional assignment that she had taken as a short-term development appointment. She had succeeded in the functional role. Even though she had significant and recent experience in operational roles, the organization would not support her move back to operations. No reasons were given other than she was valuable in the current role. She was on the verge of leaving.

Another woman had worked her way to the head of a very significant functional area. She had great credibility in what she had done and in how she was running that area. The leadership team valued her experience and expertise. They had confidence in what she was doing. However, she felt that she was equally capable to run an operational unit as any of the other candidates who had been considered in the last couple of years. She wanted the chance to try to make her contribution in a new way. The organization had not said no yet, but it had not said yes.

A positive example: An individual having held only functional positions since the early days in her career was given a chance to run a small operation to get the experience. Needless to say, she strongly believed the company supported and valued her and she was very loyal. However, the company was in substantial growth mode, the operational job had been empty for two years and no one else wanted the assignment since it was a small assignment. At least she got the experience and now holds a positive view of the organization's willingness to invest in her.

This pattern of functional roles works for and against women. On the one hand, young, talented women are recognized and often brought into exciting headquarters roles that give them access to senior people and involve them in strategic decisions. From this position, they develop a base of authority and credibility. Most of the senior women in these roles were highly respected by their male peers and had a great deal of credibility because of their expertise. They could comment in meetings from the perspective of that expertise and be heard. Many enjoyed this stature.

On the other hand, to be a CEO, most people need line experience. When the men in this study were asked if any of their female colleagues could be CEO, the answer was unequivocally, "no." When asked why, the primary reason men gave was that the women did not have the right experience (meaning P&L, operational, or client experience). The men believed that this lack of experience meant the women would not be able to be CEO because they would be less likely to be viewed as credible to the organization or to clients/customers.

Teams and Followers: The Team as a Key to Successful Performance

Women also recognize that successful performance was largely due to having a good team. They commented over and over again on the importance of their teams – relying on the collective to generate better ideas than any one person could do.

The women, almost without exception, describe their leadership style as one of collaboration and inclusion – bringing the team together; debating ideas collectively; open, honest dialogue; all voices being heard; and then reaching a conclusion on the best possible action. They also describe knowing the members of their teams personally – knowing about family or life situations, knowing what the individuals aspire to, and spending time developing the individuals.

Some men also describe their leadership style as collaborative or inclusive. However, they often note that women

52

seem too consensus-oriented. The men describe involving everyone on the team when it is an issue that is relevant to everyone, but being quite comfortable going to one or two individuals on issues for which they believe the team does not need to have input. Women may do the same, but they do not use that language in describing their work style.

One man described the following: The team-building approach is great for the company, but it takes too long for most of us. The company may be better off with that approach in three to five years. But, right now we are looking at grabbing all the opportunities we can get. We are thinking about the next six months, not three years from now. In this type of climate, the team approach is not as valued.

Another man described the situation as follows: Men "stick and move." That is, they spend just enough time chatting to build connections with colleagues so that when they need a piece of information, they can call and get what they need. The level of cooperation centers around exchanging information, not around true team work. According to this report, the women in his organization are playing a different game – one that may be good for the organization, but may not help women advance, fit in, or achieve in the short-term.

Men recognize that their female colleagues spend a lot of time developing the team. Some believe this is a positive outcome for the organization over the long haul. However, a couple noted that while this may be good for the long-term it may not be most effective in a short-term environment that is focused on delivering results fast.

One of the characteristics of the most successful leaders is versatility in leadership style – being able to flexibly move among even opposing trends.[18] The suggestion here is that under some circumstances, the natural style of women may not be the most effective. Women, like men, need to learn flexibility.

Many of the women told stories about team members who have followed them from previous positions. According to the women, and to some of the men who were in a position to comment, subordinates really valued working for their current female boss. The team generally valued her style, her openness, and her concern about them.

---

[18] R. Kaplan and R. Kaiser, "Developing Versatile Leadership", *MIT Sloan Management Review,* Summer 2003, Vol. 44 No.4, pg 19-26.

Conveying Confidence: The Role of the Boss' Support and of Feeling Valued

In some ways, the source one uses to define credibility is inevitably linked to one's self-confidence. If perceived credibility is high, usually confidence will be high. So, what disrupts confidence for women? In the interviews, several factors emerged:

- **Organizational changes,** whether from reorganization or a merger, such that previous roles and contributions were less valued.
- **Failure in getting a promotion** which was often seen as another form of de-valuation.
- **A sense of isolation.**
- **Ambiguous feedback** that does not explain the reasons for a change or provide guidance on what needs improvement.
- **Corporate downturn** where all jobs are at risk, money is tight, and there is less willingness to take risks. In these cases, women may be less likely to get new opportunities or even sustain current positions.

Inevitably, these factors come back to losing a source or base of credibility – whether that credibility is based on position, followership, performance, or expertise.

According to the men, women appear to want more support, recognition, and acknowledgement. One man, referencing an internal company study, noted that women were more likely than men in his company to be dissatisfied with the male boss' level of support even though the level of feedback was about equal between men and women. Men generally agreed with his assessment. Men note that female subordinates seem more concerned about a negative comment in a presentation, more likely to seek approval, and more concerned about not being able to get the boss' attention.

In each of the interviews, women's judgments of satisfaction and contentment with the current position corresponded to how valued they felt by the organization. If they had just received a new opportunity, felt there were other opportunities available to her, and believed senior leaders cared about her, then she was fairly content. Opportunities were often cited as a form of recognition, as well. Acknowledgement of performance was also a signal of being valued. Receiving clear, concise feedback about how to improve performance was also interpreted as a signal of investment in her and of being valued. Sometimes the level of bonus or salary was a signal, and could be construed negatively if she felt the pay was below industry average or below that of peers.

Genuineness, Accessibility, Predictability and Authenticity

The most admired senior leaders are usually described by others as conveying an image of confidence, having a strong presence, being seen as accessible to the organization and to peers, being cool, calm and collected in the face of chaos, and being authentic – true to themselves and true to their values. The same is expected of women who aspire to the very top positions. However, men noted many times that women were not conveying such images. A sense of isolation, the quality of relationships with a broad range of peers, and the sources of credibility were all likely to contribute to the perception that women are less relaxed in senior leadership positions. Three main issues emerge from these dynamics: the pressure to continually prove oneself, the need to be predictable and credible, and conveying a sense of genuineness and authenticity.

Feeling the Need to Prove Oneself

As already reported, most of the women interviewed strongly believed that they had to outperform the men in order to gain the same position. This effort, in combination with feeling isolated may lead to unexpected consequences on both sides.

A story to illustrate the point: One woman who was in a very demanding role had her male boss walk in and announce that her male colleagues did not like to work with her. To remedy the problem, he did provide her with a coach to help her improve. The coach interviewed all the peers and came back with two very consistent reports. First, the peers thought she was incredibly talented, competent and highly respected on a global scale in her area of expertise. They valued that expertise. But, second, they thought she did not listen to them. The woman reported that this was the best possible news the coach could provide because now she knew for sure that she was valued and respected by the team. She did not have to push so hard to be sure her point of view was considered, so she relaxed and let others on the team talk more. She reported finding this transition very easy. The secret ingredient for her was knowing that she was valued and respected. Eight months later, her boss again walked into her office and announced that she was the most valuable member of his team and increased her compensation to prove the point.

Another example: In this case, the woman had left the corporate world, but was enticed back because of a particular expertise. She agreed to take the job for three years on the condition that her contract clearly stated a three-year term and that if the corporation dismissed her at any point they would pay out the terms of the contract. The task she took on was extremely difficult in that it involved getting many units to change their normal operating mode. She felt she was succeeding largely because she knew she had nothing to lose and because "the guys knew she wasn't after their job." In effect, everyone could relax, including herself, and focus on the issues. Similar stories were told a few other times: when women did not care any longer if they were fired, they felt free to be themselves and they thought they were more effective.

Several CEOs noted that what distinguished very effective senior women from the rest was the ability to relax. As one CEO put it, "To be in this job everyone constantly comments on what you do and how you do it – sometimes unpleasantly in the newspaper. You have to be able to relax to be effective." He felt that senior women needed to understand that they had "made it," relax, and have a bit more fun.

Example: One man was commenting on a senior woman who had joined him on a project. He had not looked forward to working with her because she was so stiff and all business in the team meetings. However, when the two of them started working together he found that one-on-one she could relax, they could talk about business, and he could get to know her. He eventually told her that she was a completely different person one-on-one than in the group and even defended her to colleagues as a result of the project experience.

Predictability

Surprisingly, predictability as a characteristic of an effective leader emerged in the interviews. Men were asked to comment on promotion discussions where there were two strong, high-potential internal candidates: a man and a woman. The situation was described as follows: Many times the man would get the job because of various reservations about the woman such as, "she's not ready," "she's not tough enough," "she's too tough," etc. Some men admitted being part of such situations, whereas others reported having not experienced this. However, almost all felt that the men were being cautious in these situations. In effect, the findings were that men believed they knew the high-potential male candidate: how he would react, how he thought, what he was likely to do in a various situations, and how to persuade him. These beliefs could have been founded on experience with the male candidate or they could simply be based on believing the male candidate was like them. Either way, the predictability of the male candidate made him seem less risky. That is the catch. Leaders often prefer to staff with people who are like them. In this way, leaders know what to expect, they can trust the selected individual to make the same decision they would make, and decisions take less time when everyone thinks alike. Thus, women continue to be excluded – particularly in cases where the stakes and pressures are high.

If this summary represents anything close to reality for women seeking a high level promotion, then it further reinforces the need to build broader networks, to interact more often with male colleagues, to let down some (not all) barriers so that colleagues and bosses can have a better sense of how the woman will react. Accordingly, if a woman is seen as more predictable, then the organization is more likely to take a risk on her and to provide the developmental opportunities for her to gain credibility and develop self-confidence.

Authenticity and Genuineness
Two characteristics emerged from interviews with the women who were content with their roles in the corporation: foremost was their overwhelming sense of being able to be

themselves, to laugh at themselves, to not have to be "like the men;" and secondly, at the same time, there was a feeling that gender was not a factor – they reported not thinking about being a woman. Their male colleagues echoed both of these characteristics. Men also commented that the women they considered most effective were at ease, able to relax, and could use humor to their advantage. The men also noted that they did not think about these particular women as being "women," rather they saw them as colleagues like all other colleagues. Finding tactics and role models will likely be a critical factor in women learning to be more genuine, more themselves in the corporate world.

In summary, the ability of women to be authentic, to relax, and to convey confidence and presence are critical for achieving higher positions.

Perceived Sense of Isolation

Again, in some ways, little has changed over the last twenty-five years with the experiences of corporate women. There have been subtle changes, though. Twenty-five years ago, women noted the challenges of being the first and only woman in a position, the difficulties of living within the "male" norms of behavior, and the challenges of being an executive and still coming home to prepare dinner and take care of their children. Those core issues are still present though their form has varied as we will see below. The constant is the continued sense of isolation. The belief in how easy it will be to change that sense of isolation has changed and some of the ways of adapting have subtle nuances. The things that contribute to a sense of isolation today include:

- Being **the first, the only**, or the youngest woman.
- Adherence to a perceived **narrow band of acceptable behavior**.
- The declining **proportion of women** as one climbs the hierarchy.
- Not believing one's **voice** is heard.
- An approach to decision-making that relies on **open, team debate and discussion**.
- The pressures of **family** life.

First and Only

For almost all of the women in this study, they were the first woman in a position and/or the only woman on the team. For some, there were occasions in which they had one female colleague on the team for a short time in their career. There are very few cases in which a woman had two or more female colleagues.

In addition, for almost all of the women in this study, not only were they the first and only woman, they were also nearly always the youngest on the team.

The net result was a sense of being special and unique along with a sense of being different and alone (cf., *Breaking the Glass Ceiling,* 1987, 1992). The most commonly cited example was being the only one in the toilet while watching the men go off together and continue the conversation.

An additional burden is the sense of visibility. Since they were the first or the only, the women felt every move they made was watched and critiqued far more than it would have been for men. In ways this meant they had an advantage because they were closely watched, so positive outcomes were more likely to be noticed. On the other hand, their mistakes followed them for years – ten years in one woman's case and irrespective of all the other positive outcomes she had delivered since. One man described the situation this way: "As senior leaders, we know that any time we put a woman into a role, she will be very visible. Therefore, she better be superb or else we run the risk that we (as leaders) will look bad for making that selection. She is visible and so are we for making the choice. You scrutinize a candidate much more closely when you think the choice will be so closely watched."

Most women reported enjoying the visibility. For some, particularly those over forty, the visibility becomes less enjoyable and more burdensome over the years.

As one author writes,[19] nothing a woman wears is ever neutral. For men, certain attire is neutral, not worthy of comment and just like everyone else. For women, because there are so few of them, nothing is neutral.

One woman described the following: Everything you did was noticed and discussed from what you wore to what you ate. As soon as I wore a red dress, I could watch women throughout the organization copy what I wore. If I wore a dress, my male peers would comment on what it meant that I was wearing a dress. If I wore pants, they would comment on the implications on my wearing pants. It got old.

Narrow Band of Behavior

All corporations and all senior leadership groups have an unstated set of acceptable behaviors – things such as attire (e.g., color and style of ties or shoes), the expression of emotion, particularly anger, (e.g., whether emotion is tolerated or not, what expressions of anger are permitted and when), what the group does to socialize (e.g., sports talk, golf, hunting, fishing). In the 80's and 90's, women were held to a narrower set of standards in order to be accepted at the senior levels (Breaking the Glass Ceiling, 1987, 1992). For many that meant never expressing anger, for example. Or, as

---

[19] G. Evans, *Play Like a Man, Win Like a Woman*, 2000; D. Tannen, *Talking 9 to 5*, 1994.

one woman described – once in her career she pounded the table and shouted as the men typically did. Her point was heard and she was not punished for the outbreak. However, she also knew she could only do it once in her career.

For about half of the women in this study, the narrower band of acceptable behavior still applied. They believed they could not get away with the same behavior as the men. They believed they are held to a narrower range and a narrower set of standards.

However, the other half believed the exact opposite. That is, they believed they could get away with behaviors that would not be tolerated for men. Many of these women stated that at one point in their careers they believed they had to adhere to a narrower standard; however, today they felt the standard was probably more self-imposed than reality. The most commonly cited example was again regarding dress – the ability to wear a broader range of clothing and to express individual style in items such as jewelry, leather, fish net stockings, and so forth. With regards to the expression of anger, these women felt that they could express anger just as the men did, but, they also acknowledged that they would not do so because this was inconsistent with their style.

Examples

While many women noted that the corporation was doing far fewer social events than a decade ago and that these events tended to be more sensitive to varied interests, there were still plenty of stories about women "going along" with activities that were not to their liking. The most outlandish of those stories follows: A woman on a senior team was leaving the corporation. Her boss wanted to throw a party to celebrate her time with the company and her contributions. The boss decided that the party should be a weekend hunting expedition to some remote region. That's what the group did... the woman joined them though she was not and never had been a hunter.

On the other hand, other women are feeling more comfortable saying they will not join such expeditions: A senior team decided that they needed a team-building event. There was one woman on the team. The group suggested that they go on a fishing expedition for the weekend, again in a distant location. The woman initially agreed so that she could go and be part of the team. However, shortly before the event, she decided this was not a comfortable position for her and she respectfully declined to join them. The team accepted her choice, seemingly without repercussions.

The Proportions of Women

The numbers in the senior team ranks are still very low – as stated in the beginning of this report, less than 13%, depending upon the country; that is, at best 1 in a team of 7 or 8, 2 in a team of 14 or more.

For most senior teams and for most of the women in this study, this means that they had one female colleague at best for a period of time. As one woman observed, "You could watch the women come and go. As soon as one entered the team, one would be exited in one way or another fairly soon. You knew that there was a younger replacement waiting in the wings when the next one exited. There was a seat for one woman, not for two, at the senior leadership level. You knew you were the next to go as soon as you entered the role."

Voice

Women still report that they struggle to get heard – some more so than others, some more so earlier in their career than now. Some believe this occurs because their voice is quiet and their stature is petite. Some are unwilling to pound the table (or the verbal equivalent) to gain recognition. Some report that it is not their style to see who can shout the loudest in order to be heard. The vast majority of the women in this study found getting their voice heard to be a challenge. Half still report this to be a challenge; half have

68

found strategies to manage the challenge. For example, several have found that not speaking can be as effective as talking the loudest; they find that when they do speak, people tend to listen attentively. A few reported having bosses who made sure the team stopped to listen to the woman who had just joined them and thus ensured that the team adopted an inclusive style.

Almost all of the women recognize that their ideas are often attributed to male colleagues. For some this is not an issue as long as the idea is implemented and the company comes to the best solution. Others will find ways to remind the group where the idea originated – whether with humor or not (e.g., "I am glad you agree with the idea I suggested.") (cf., *Breaking the Glass Ceiling,* 1987, 1992).

Debate and Discussion

Here, there are two very different sets of experiences. On the one hand, many women report believing that issues should be brought up with their peers on the leadership team: all the facts should be placed on the table; there should be an honest, open debate about the issues and the options; an agreement should be reached; and everyone should execute against that agreement as soon as the debate is concluded. Women generally report that they prefer this style and finding environments that encourage that type of open debate most satisfying.

69

On the other hand, some women recognize that this is not an effective use of time. These women note that men often operate quite differently. They will talk with individuals in the team one-on-one to learn their perspective. They will weigh all the opinions in advance of bringing the issue to the team. When the issue is brought to the team, it is presented as a recommendation with only the necessary supporting facts and the presentation is done in such a way to allow the team to see the logic of accepting the recommendation offered. Not much time is spent in debate during the team meeting. Facts that have been dismissed for one reason or another are not discussed.

One woman noted: Women shoot themselves in the foot when they make presentations to the senior leadership team. They bring in all the pros and cons of an issue and expect to discuss those, whereas the men bring a recommendation and provide only the facts that support that recommendation. Facts that are counter are omitted.

Another woman noted: In evaluating peers, women were much more candid, direct and open – offering balanced perspectives about both strengths and weaknesses. However, when men evaluate peers, particularly if they like the peer, then they only discuss strengths, assuming everyone knows that any candidate has weaknesses. In this way, the men are not calling attention to the negatives. Instead, they are offering a positive perspective that sounds like an endorsement. The balanced perspectives of women can be viewed as a lack of endorsement or as a question about capability.

It is not clear whether one style of dealing with discussion and recommendations is more effective than another, or whether styles differ by level in the organization or by complexity of the issue. There has been much written about the more tentative language of women noting that women speak in ways that encourage the sharing of opinions.[20] In addition, there is a good bit of evidence from child development studies to support the notion that young girls seek patterns of play that continue engagement either within the group or with adults, whereas young boys are not at all concerned

---

[20] D. Tannen, *Talking 9 to 5*, 1994.

with continued engagement.[21] Thus, some have argued that women, in general, are more inclined than men to seek collaboration in a variety of ways. The purpose here is not to argue that women have one style and men have another. There is probably nothing that precludes one style over the other, and, there is no evidence that one style versus another is more effective or more advantageous for an organization. Instead, the issue for women and for organizations is more a matter of expectations.

Regardless of the preferences or predispositions, if an organization is expecting one set of behaviors from a senior leader but is getting another set of behaviors, then that leader, male or female, will not be evaluated highly. For example, one CEO described a woman who reported to him a couple of years earlier. According to his report she was very difficult to work with because she wanted the debate to continue long after everyone else had already made up their minds. Her behavior may have been inappropriate or it may have been simply different. Either way, it was labeled as inappropriate and she was eventually demoted from the senior team.

---

[21] E. Maccoby, "Gender and Relationships: A Developmental Account", *American Psychologist*, April 1990, pg 513-520; C. Eckerman and S. Didow, "Toddlers' Social Coordinations: Changing Responses to Another's Invitation to Play", *Developmental Psychology*, Vol. 25. No. 5, 1989.

Family

Breaking the Glass Ceiling (1987, 1992) reported that women struggle with being a breadwinner and having a spouse believe that dinner still magically appears on the table. For many women in the corporate world this is probably still the case. However, for the women in this sample, it does not appear to be an issue. Almost all of the women with children have husbands who have sufficiently flexible schedules and who can come home to manage household duties or pick up the children. All of these women said that the job would not be possible if the spouse was not at home or flexible. They all recognize that to do the job at this level, a couple must have adequate household help and that the couple alone can probably not manage kids and two equally demanding careers. These women felt, by and large, that they had found a way to manage the role as a mother and could live with the choices they were making.

However, the men who were interviewed believed that the single biggest challenge for women in senior leadership positions was the pull from family.

As one man described, "The pull for a woman to be home when something happens to a child is far greater than for a man. Even if the spouse is home with the child and she knows the child is well cared for, she still feels the need to be home with the child. That would never occur to me. It just wouldn't be a part of my consideration set."

Men recognized that young children typically want mom and not necessarily dad, and that the burden of being a mother was greater than that of being a dad in spite of the best of help and the best of efforts.

This stereotype of women being mothers and breadwinners was recently captured in the novel, *I Don't Know How She Does It.*[22] The story describes a female investment banker who holds a senior position and lives with the constant pull of being a mother -- so much so that she would re-decorate store-bought cupcakes for her daughter to take to school so that the appearance of making them at home would be maintained. Judging from the number of women interviewed for this study who had read the novel and fully identified with the experience of the female character, for some the pull is as strongly felt as ever even if the current household arrangements seem to work well.

Men also recognized that mothers worry regularly about be-ing away from the kids – they hear their female colleagues talking about it. One noted that men talk about children as do women – but men talk about how the child did in the soccer game, whereas women talk about being away from the children.

---

[22]A. Pearson, *I Don't Know How She Does It,* 2003.

There is a hidden danger here. To the extent that organizations believe women will not be able to take a new assignment because of family, they are less likely to offer women the option. Men admit that this is the case and they admit that the same occurs for men who also cannot move or assume more responsibility because of family. Where the burden lies in ensuring that women have opportunities is worthy of debate. This discussion needs to occur in organizations, in women's networks, and with high-potential talent. The point is that organizations need to understand family "pulls" for both men and for women and how those affect career choices. Furthermore, the choice to take any assignment should be seen as an individual choice at a given point in time, not one for which the answer should be assumed for women, or for men, or generalized across populations.

While we might all recognize that the top jobs have become almost impossible to do without a 24/7 commitment, and we might wish that the corporate world could move to a more reasonable demand on time, this is not likely to happen anytime soon for two reasons. First, as long as there are more people who want the top job than there are positions available, someone will always be willing to put in whatever effort is required to get the job done. In that way, the tournament will continue. Second, the pressures for corporate performance are not likely to decline. One man commented: "It is a nice idea. But, we simply cannot return to a more costly, less productive way of working. Our clients demand that we work as they do. We have to maintain or even improve our progress in controlling costs, we have to continue doing as much or more with less, and we will probably have to cut costs and increase productivity even more in coming years." Or as stated by another person: "The CEO's wife regularly comments that as long as her husband is the CEO, his time belongs to the company, not to her." Thus, it is unlikely that the senior-most jobs will become less demanding anytime soon.

Back at the Beginning - A Perceived Sense of Isolation

The comment mentioned over and over again from the women who had left the corporate world or who were con- sidering leaving was the overwhelming sense of isolation. One woman made the following comment: "I watch my peers. They always come to meetings in twos and threes. But I always come as one." Several women who were considering leaving, noted that apart from one or two subordinates and maybe a peer, they would not really miss seeing anyone they worked with when (or if) they left. One woman in a board position noted that at the board level, the sense of isolation was even worse.

The experience of women may or may not be qualitatively different from that of men, however, many of the women I interviewed were troubled by their own sense of isolation.

This sense of isolation made all the other challenges of the corporate world more difficult. Even women recognized the need to have fun in the face of all the challenges. From all of the above discussions, a set of factors have merged which in any number of combinations would create a sense of isolation. And in turn, the sense of isolation compounds all the other factors.

If we accept the stereotype that women are good at relationships or strive to build deeper relationships or get a sense of self-worth from being strongly connected to people, then we can imagine why the isolation is so distressing. Contributing factors: less breadth of exposure to people across the business, fewer peer-to-peer relationships, little social interaction, weak relationships with bosses, being unique and highly visible, being promoted out of cycle with peers (either above or behind), not participating in speculative discussions about the business, staying focused on the task at hand, or having a different approach to leading a team or to engaging in debate. Any number of these would leave any leader feeling out of step with the organization – isolated and less effective except in her area of expertise. To increase the number of women who stay in the corporate world, we have to tackle the enormous sense of isolation that women are feeling.

Part 4

Why Women Leave and Stay in the Corporate World

The Popular Press Stories

Articles in *Business Week*, *Fortune Magazine* and the *New York Times* have highlighted women "stepping out" and "dropping out," just as they reach the highest rungs of the corporate ladder. According to the Center for Women's Business Research, a woman leaves corporate America every 11 seconds.[23]

There have been a number of highly publicized cases including: Marta Carbrera of JPMorganChase, Mary Lou Quinlan of N.W.Ayer,[24] Colonel Lois Beard of the U.S. Army,[25] and Christine Lucci of Citigroup Germany.[26] These executives are choosing to exit at the point when their experience, knowledge and

---

[23] H.Shea, "People Tell Their Stories: Work Related Challenges", www.lifechallenges.org, cited July 9, 2004.

[24] L. Tischer, "Where are the Women?" *Fast Company*, February 2004, pg 52-60.

[25] E. Becker, "Motherhood Deters Women from Army's Highest Ranks", *The New York Times,* November 29, 1999.

[26] P. Jenkins, "Citigroup Loses Top Banker in Germany," *Financial Times,* May 25, 2004.

credibility as role models are at a peak and when they can make significant contributions to the organization.

The situation in Europe is no different. In the U.K., a recent survey conducted by the British Market Research Bureau found that women are slightly more likely than men to "downshift," that is, to change to a lower paying job to reduce work hours.[27] Unilever's CEO, Niall Fitzgerald, has stated that at Unilever women are recruited at equal numbers to men, but the percentages drop dramatically at the upper echelons despite significant efforts within the company.[28] An MBA education does not make much difference either. A Harvard study of 902 women who received MBAs between 1971 and 1981 found that 25% of women who earned MBAs in the 1970's have left the corporate work force.[29] More recently, a survey of female Harvard Business School graduates from the classes of 1971, 1985, and 1991 reported that only 38% of female graduates were working full-time.[30]

---

[27] A. Fifield, "Desire to Trade Pressure for Peace Grows", *Financial Times,* November 25, 2003, pg 4.

[28] *Financial Times,* June 16, 2003.

[29] C.D. Sutton & K.K. Moore, "Executive Women – 20 Years Later, *Harvard Business Review*, 1985, pg 42-66.

[30] L. Belkin, "The Opt-Out Revolution", *The New York Times Magazine,* October 26, 2003.

Contrary to popular views, not all of these women are leaving to be home with the family. Eve-olution, a U.K based company, reports that less than 20% of the women leaving corporate jobs in the U.K. do so for family reasons.[31]

Many of the women who are leaving corporate jobs are starting their own businesses. According to the Center for Women's Business Research, more than 50% of the 10.4 million privately held businesses in the U.S. are owned by women. For the past twenty years, women-owned firms have grown at almost twice the rate of other firms.[32] In a study of 800 men and women business owners, 44% of the women report starting their own business because of an entre-preneurial idea or because they believed they could independently do what they were doing at their former corporations.[33]

---

[31] L. Reynolds, "Why Women are Leaving Successful Careers: A Male Perspective". *Eve-olution Newsletter,* December 2003, www.eve-olution.net.

[32] Top Facts About Women–Owned Businesses". Center for Women's Business Research, http://www.cfwbr.org/facts/index.php,

[33] "Paths to Entrepreneurship: New Directions for Women in Business", prepared by Catalyst and the National Foundation for Women Business Owners, February, 1998, www.c200.org/externa/ research, cited July 9, 2004.

The Reasons for Exiting: Current Myths

In a report by Catalyst on women in European businesses, 64% of women respondents (49% of men respondents) say that not having senior female role models is a barrier to women's advancement in European organizations.[34] Thus, the exodus of senior women has multiple impacts on corporate efforts to diversify.

In addition, the search for balance in life is part of the concern for everyone in the corporate world. In a survey of women and men in corporate roles, Hakim reports that men and women want some sort of balance in their lives but women slightly more so: 55% of men are totally career-obsessed versus 3% for women.[35]

Furthermore, disturbing new trends in work/life balance seems to be emerging. According to Hewlett, female executives are not managing to have a career and a family. Among women in the U.S. who are earning more than $65,000 in a large corporate job and who are between the ages of 41 and 55, 33% were childless and 40% were not married. These

---

[34] "Women in Leadership: A European Business Imperative", Catalyst Publication, www.catalystwomen.org/publications/summaries.htm, cited July 9, 2004.

[35] Interview with Catherine Hakim, *Fast Company,* 2004, http://www.fastcompany.com/articles/2004/01/hakim.html, cited July 9, 2004.

women carried the large proportion of household responsibilities.[36]

Clearly, women who have children feel the pressures of being a mother and managing a household. These cannot be ruled out. In a controversial article, *Time* reported on several women who were pulled between the pressures of work and the demands of family and who were choosing to stay at home with kids.[37] However, there are also cases of executive women leaving when there are no obvious family pressures. Furthermore, as women leave corporate jobs, they often start small companies that demand similar (or greater) time commitments as did the corporate job. Finally, several senior women have husbands who are at home or whose work is flexible enough to permit the husband to manage the inevitable household challenges.[38]

Thus, not all of the reasons for the departure of women from the corporate world can be laid on the challenges of raising a family and working. As we shall see later in this report, many senior executive women feel that by this point in their

---

[36] S.A. Hewlett, "Executive Women and the Myth of Having it All," *Harvard Business Review,* April 2002, pg 66-73.

[37] C. Wallis, "The Case for Staying Home," *Time,* March 22, 2004, pg 51-62.

[38] B. Morris, "Trophy Husbands," *Fortune,* September 27, 2002.

careers, they have come to terms with the balancing act of work and home and have found the means to manage that balance reasonably well.

Even more disturbing and controversial, recent reports indicate that women are not succeeding in gaining senior roles because they are not as ambitious as men or not as driven to succeed as men.[39] This report is in direct contrast to the reports from coaches who run assessment centers. Typically, they report finding a greater need for achievement via self-actualized, independent means (as opposed to conformance means) among executive women than among executive men as measured by the California Psychological Inventory.[40]

Other recent articles report that women in management positions spend less time at work;[41] however, most of these

---

[39] A. Fels, "Do Women Lack Ambition?", *Harvard Business Review*, April, 2004, pg 50-60.

[40] Personal conversation with Dr. Randall P. White, July 11, 2004.

[41] "Beyond Good Intentions: Creating Organizations Where Women Thrive and Contribute Fully", *It's About Time,* Spring 2002, Vol 6, research brief from WFD Consulting (46 hours for women, 48 hours for men). L. Tischer, "Where are the Women?" *Fast Company*, February 2004, pg 52-60 (40.4 hours for women vs. 46.1 for men based on US Bureau of Labor Statistics).

summaries are based on Bureau of Labor statistics. These statistics combine Social Security records for all occupational groups in the U.S. with no regard for executive rank. Thus, these reports most likely have little bearing on the departure rates of senior executive women.

The situation is more complex than any of the above myths have implied. None of the myths seems to have uniform applicability. Nor do any of them seem to explain the exodus of senior women who have had very successful careers.

During the interviews, several causes of frustration stood out, such as believing they were not making a sufficient contribution, their unique skills were not valued, being in the impossible spotlight into which senior women are placed, playing the politics and power games and fitting into the network. Each of these seems to take a cumulative toll.

Clearly for all the efforts to date and the discussions about increasing the number of senior women in corporations, we seem to have made only modest progress. The belief in the need for diversity is as strong as ever in the U.S., U.K., and Europe. The lack of talented women in senior roles also seems to have a significant impact on corporations. Yet, we know little more than popular press versions about why senior women are choosing to exit. Therefore, the focus of this research report is to understand more about women's experiences at senior levels and why so many are interested in exiting after fruitful careers, at relatively young ages, and with much more to contribute. The loss in human capital for corporations and the loss of senior female role models are tremendous.

Reports from Women Interviewed

Why women are leaving

Women Who Left Corporate Roles

Of the 64 interviews, 11 had already left the corporate world at the time of the interview. The women who left corporate roles report a varied set of reasons for choosing to leave. No single reason is common to all the departures; rather, there is a rich collection of factors that in various combinations contribute to each decision. That tapestry includes the following issues:

- ***Not getting a sought-after promotion*** (or increased level of responsibility) and being told that she had gone as far as she could go within the corporation. Usually this came with little to no prior feedback on performance (pro or con), no explicit reason for why she would not go further, and a self-reported history of a great track record on performance to date.

- ***A change in the organizational climate***

  o Seeing the political tides change and believing that she would not be able to accomplish the agenda she had set in taking a particular role -- meaning she believed she would not be able to do what she came to the job to do. Sometimes this occurred because a particular boss was no longer at the corporation. More often it occurred because the power base at the top of the organization shifted, and as a result her access shifted, as did the agenda.

  o A change in the culture such that the current climate was not positive and no longer worth the effort required of the job. This is typically described as a cli-mate where it is every person for himself/herself and it does not matter how you get the numbers so long as you get them – performance drove everything.

  o A merger opportunity that created a good exit package – in all of these cases though, the plan to exit had been created years before and the merger provided a window of opportunity.

- **Being driven out** – usually from a change in senior leadership, followed by a series of decisions to change the reporting structure with the net result that the person's position/contribution was diminished, decreased in rank, or devalued.

One woman watched all of her female peers exit the corporation and noted that the same pattern happened to men; however she noted that the men were given titles that denoted appropriate status even if the role was less significant and/or that the men were not alone – meaning that many other male peers with whom they could commiserate were in the same position. According to her report, this was not true for her female peers, and as a result the women felt alone and isolated. Eventually all of these women left.

- **Not having as much fun as they used to** – either because the business changed, the peer set changed, the job changed, or the demands changed.
- **Needing a hiatus to "defuse"**[42] and re-think the next chapter. For most, the opportunity to make a greater contribution to society was a strong theme.

---

[42] The general report so far is that individuals need 8 to 12 months before they feel de-fused and can even think about next steps. The recommendation from the women themselves has been to be cautious about how much one takes on in that first year.

- ***Personal goals were achieved*** so there was no longer a reason to stay in the job just to prove to themselves or to the rest of the world that they could do it.

- ***Children were a factor though not the only factor*** for two people. Each of these is unique. In one case, the woman did not want to take on the tasks and commit the hours that would be required at the next level, nor did she want to force her family into yet another move. In the other case, the woman had done enough, proven enough, and wanted to do something different, something that made a contribution, and something that gave her time with her family.

To summarize, women who left the corporate world did so largely because they no longer found the job exciting or challenging. They did not like the current corporate culture or at least the culture created by their boss. They were tired of the political games. As one woman stated, "You break so many glass ceilings on the way up that you finally come to realize you have accumulated a lot of shards along the way."

At the time of the interviews, all eleven women had been out of the corporate world from less than a month to three years. All seemed delighted with the choice they had made. Six reported no desire to ever return to the large corporate world. One of the eleven has taken a job in another large corporation. Four of the eleven were taking time to re-evaluate and were unsure about what they wanted to do next – non-profit, own business, or small business versus another large corporate job. All eleven still felt they had a significant contribution to make. All of the women wanted to consider other ways of making a contribution to the society rather than through the corporate world.

An observation:

Women seem to fare well and enjoy being in organizations where:

1. Performance is fairly evaluated and rewarded.
2. The organization is in a growth mode and there are more opportunities than there are capable leaders.
3. The organization has grown dramatically through a series of acquisitions and no one knows each other well.
4. There is a strong culture of pulling together and collaborating to solve problems.

Women seem not to fare well or enjoy the experience when:

1. The organization goes through a down cycle so that jobs are cut and leaders tend to resort to individuals they know well to run various components of the business.

2. There is a merger and a competition for a limited number of positions.
3. Individuals running the organization have known each other for a long time.

The Women Who Considered Leaving

Of the 64 interviews, 53 were still in the corporate world at the time of the interview. These women were asked whether or not they were happy, content, and satisfied with their current positions and whether or not they were considering leaving. Their responses were as follows:

45% (24 out of 53) were content and were not looking to leave the corporate world.

32% (16 out of 53) were currently thinking about leaving.

25% (13 out of 53) had thought about leaving sometime over the last three to five years.

For the women who had or were considering leaving, the reasons were very clear and not very different from those who had already left the corporate world. The perspectives included the following:

* *Being bored with the job* – having been in the role for over three or four years, having learned all there was to learn and either not seeing or not being given the chance at new opportunities. Each felt they had

91

much more to contribute than the organization was taking advantage of. Each felt they had a proven track record of performance.

- **Organizational climate** – dissatisfaction with the current direction of the organization, the choices being made by senior leaders vis-à-vis customers, rewards, promotions, business opportunities, and leadership style.
- **A sense of isolation** – feeling alone and disconnected in combination with not having as much fun as in the past. Many of these women felt that they were one person inside the organization and a different person outside.
- **A desire to do something worthwhile for society** – something that made more of a contribution than "further increasing shareholder value."
- **Family** was only mentioned as a factor after some set of the above factors became significant. Several noted that by the time one reaches the senior ranks, one has learned to manage family or home issues.
- **Not feeling valued by the organization**

The reasons women left and the reasons women consider leaving were pretty much the same. The differences really seem to be ones of magnitude: something happens to heighten the sense of frustration (e.g., the same type of event has happened too many times), an external event drives serious consideration (e.g., a death), or there is an opportunity for a favorable exit package. Those who are considering leaving but haven't left yet are still holding out hoping that something will change soon.

Why Women Are Staying

Slightly more than a third of the women, 36% (23 of the 64) were not considering leaving the corporation. Many of these women had just received a promotion or an increase in responsibility. They were delighted with the new opportunity and were excited about the challenge. In many ways, the new challenges can be seen as either a source of acceptance and value by the organization, as well as a source of renewal for the individual.

The most unique attribute of these women was their comfort level with the male culture of the organization and a confidence in their own style. By and large, this group had not become "masculine" or "more male than the men;" rather, they had learned how to fit their own style into the male dominated culture in a way that was comfortable to them.

One of the observations that emerged from interviews with both men and women was a dislike of women who were more male than the men. In one organization, all of the early female pioneers who were "more male than the men" had left (by one means or another). The organization (both men and women) was now pleased with the style women leaders were exhibiting – strong, driven and opinionated, yet not afraid of being feminine in dress and in style. Men also reported enjoying female colleagues who could be themselves in the office.

Examples from Women Who Are Staying: One person reported liking sports, enjoyed talking about sports, liked being around men, and created opportunities to build social networks by hosting poker parties.

Another was comfortable letting men talk about themselves and their jobs. She used that receptivity to strategically get male colleagues to talk about their jobs and what was on their minds. In her experience, those opportunities provided a great deal of learning and strategic insight as well as helped build relationships.

One woman decided years prior to her current senior position to understand and lead by her own style and to use that style to push forward new visions. That style has worked to her advantage in creating a new business model. What distinguishes her is her comfort level with her style and herself as a woman. Her style can be characterized as being very inclusive, open to the opinions of others, willing to take significant risks and willing to let the team run most of the business while she focuses on the things that only she can do. She also makes significant efforts to develop the team to the point where they can function without her day-to-day input.

One woman had a strong sense of self-confidence that came from knowing she had nothing to lose. She could walk away at any moment with a great financial standing after having done more than she had ever hoped to do. The net result is that she is willing to say what she thinks and not worry about how she is perceived.

For another, an early mentor in her career who came from outside her firm, demonstrated to her and coached her on how to walk the balance of being feminine and trust her own style while also being powerful and effective as a leader.

A Comparison of Leavers, Considerers, and Stayers

There are no obvious ways in which those who choose to leave the corporation (Leavers), those who consider leaving (Considerers), and those choosing to stay (Stayers) differ. As the chart below shows, age, marital status, children at home, or a spouse in the corporate world really does not substantially differ between the groups.

	Leavers	Considerers	Stayers
Average age	49.4 yrs	44.9 yrs	45.6 yrs
% who are married	82%	76.9%	95%
% with children at home	50%	44.8%	50%
% with husbands in corporate world	33.3%	20%	18.75%
% in general management roles	36.4%	37.5%	39.3%

Regional and Industry Differences

There were no noticeable differences between the reports of women in the U.S., U.K. or other countries in Europe. There were also no noticeable differences between the reports of women from one industry versus another.

Is The Experience Any Different For Men?
In describing the reasons women were leaving, many of the twenty-six men who were interviewed recognized that this set of experiences was no different for men in the organization.

However, there are some important distinctions. One, the men who struggle with these same issues are also not getting promoted to the top of the organization, just as women are not going any higher.

Two, men from the U.S. and Europe who choose corporate careers seem to have more of their self-worth tied to the status of holding a job in a large corporation. They are breadwinners, but so are the women in this study. Therefore, it appears not to be the financial burdens that keep men in corporate jobs, but status or the pursuit of a dream or ideal.[43]

---

[43] R. Mintz, *The Scripts We Live By: How Individuation, Proteanism and Narrative Disruption Relate to Personal Transformation & Renewal*, Dissertation at Fielding Institute, 2003; H. Levinson, *Seasons of a Man's Life*, 1978.

Three, although men's careers take negative turns as well, the men are usually part of a larger cohort group that is experiencing the same effect, thus, they may not feel singled out or isolated.

Four, there are no easy opportunities for men to make a contribution outside of the traditional job. They are often not as connected to the broader non-profit world as women appear to be, and they may not see as many external leadership opportunities as women see. There are few role models for men leaving corporations to work in schools or the arts – or at least none appear in the popular press.

Five, it has become acceptable, almost fashionable, for women to consider leaving – the very discussion would have labeled a woman as a drop-out among her professional friends twenty-five years ago. Today, it is almost a rank of distinction, and the reason why is not at all clear.

Summary

In short, women are choosing to leave because they are not gaining positions in which they can continue to grow and learn. Once the personal growth appears to come to an end, then all the other factors weigh on the choice to stay or leave – enjoyment, collegiality with peers, politics, changes in the corporate climate, or the pull from family. In these cases, retaining women would involve continuing to provide new opportunities for growth and valuing the contributions that are made.

For women who are not gaining the positions that provide growth and learning, the situations are often very complex with three alternative explanations:

1) **Politics:** resulting from the inevitable changes that come in the chess game at the top of any organization, from the series of re-organizations that all corporations go through, or from being outside the prevailing network.

2) **Derailment:** resulting from weakened performance that had never been discussed, overdependence on a single boss/mentor, behavioral issues that are never tackled, and so forth.

3) **Experience**: resulting from holding a limited range of positions throughout one's career, most often in headquarters or in staff roles and lacking operational experience.

Example: One senior woman confided after a very trying week that headhunter calls were becoming more and more tempting. In her organization, she had been touted by peers as an example of a very successful, highly respected, talented leader in a line position who was delivering great results. Her peers valued her and assumed she would be a successor to her boss. However, in private, more senior level members of the organization had doubts about her skills for the next level. Yet, no one was talking with her about their concerns. Thus, she had no opportunity to develop capability or to show she actually had the right capabilities. In effect, she was being judged against a set of criteria for which she had no clue that she needed to prove herself. Whether she had the capability or not, we may never know. The point is that she was not being given the opportunity.

At times in the interviews it was hard to tell whether the lack of opportunities occurred because women were easier targets during times of change, whether bosses just want to bring in a protégé or a close member of a former team, or whether the women's leadership was lacking in some dimension. In one illustrative case, the woman and the organization held diametrically opposing views of her performance – it is impossible to know which side was more accurate.

Regardless of the "real" reasons, organizations and women leaders need to be aware of potential moves that can force senior women out of roles. Where performance is not up to standards on any dimension, feedback needs to be delivered clearly with appropriate developmental support.

Part 5

Recommendations

The underlying issues that affect women and encourage their departures from organizations are not simple – they are subtle and they are strongly interdependent. Organizations have taken many actions from instituting flexible work schedules to recruiting efforts to supporting women's networks. All of these actions probably have positive outcomes for some. Nevertheless, to truly grow the ranks of senior women, organizations, bosses, and the women themselves need to take a stronger look at the subtleties that drive results. Both need a deep, honest consideration of how these play out in the current organization. These subtleties cluster around five themes which can be a source for discussion within the organization:

- The **sense of isolation** that women feel and the reasons for that sense of isolation in the current organization
- The **sources of credibility** for women in the organization – the value placed on performance and the style of delivering that performance, experience across the organization, expertise as a base of credi-

101

bility, and experience in line and operational roles. Both women and the organization need to consider how each value the sources of credibility, how they prefer to develop those sources, and the barriers for development.

- The **quality, depth and breadth of organizational relationships** – the barriers or opportunities for developing these relationships
- The **centrality of a boss** – the need to receive honest, direct feedback; the need to have a mentor, sponsor, coach, and advocate; the need for more than one such boss in a career; and the ability to develop a good relationship with a new boss
- The **ability to be authentic** – to relax, to be themselves, to be genuine, to be approachable, to have presence

In the interviews in this research, a few key themes appear that suggest immediate actions. These actions are organized by what the organization, the boss, and the women can do to increase retention and effectiveness.

Questions and Actions for the Organization
- *Developmental Assignments* – Women leave or start considering departure when they cannot see continued opportunities for growth and advancement. Many factors may drive the ultimate choice to stay or leave,

but the lack of opportunity starts the cycle of questioning. Carefully examine how long women are in positions and track opportunities for high-potential women the organization wants to retain. Talented women are in short supply across almost all organizations and they are easily recruited to another corporation if given the right opportunity for advancement.

- o Where are the best developmental jobs for senior leadership positions?
- o Are women in those jobs, why or why not?
- o What support would the organization have to offer to "virtually guarantee" that taking a risk on a woman in one of those positions would be successful?
- o Are women in assignments of longer duration than male peers in comparable roles?
- o Are individuals (women and men) given the opportunity to accept or reject an assignment, or are the choices made for them without consulting them because of assumptions about current life situations?

- *Feedback* – Women by and large are not getting the honest feedback they need to develop into the most senior positions. They often do not have a clear, concise picture of how the organization sees them, their leadership, and their capabilities. Thus they do

103

not have the opportunity to develop or to show their skills.

- o Do performance review processes include specific behavioral feedback as well as honest performance feedback?
- o Talent managers can facilitate the process of helping women get the feedback they need to ensure success. This can be done with an outside coaching resource or an internal resource depending upon the structure and culture of the organization.

- *"Godfathering"* – Women seldom get the mentoring, sponsoring, advocacy, coaching, "godfathering" that typically turns great male executives into superb strategic thinkers and great leaders.
  - o Are talented women receiving the necessary godfathering from senior leaders and/or from the board?
  - o While outside mentoring can certainly help, it will not provide the insight on internal politics or the necessary advocacy.
  - o Consider a developmental advisor – someone from senior ranks who is not the boss and who is in a different line of business. The DA can serve as a mentor, advocate and coach. In some cases the relationship that develops will

be a close one but not in all. Companies that use the concept of a DA recognize that everyone on the senior team is responsible for helping to identify and develop talented leaders of the future.

- *Operational Experience* – Women are still not getting the operational experience which is critical at senior levels regardless of the position or the function. Even functional heads today benefit greatly from line and operational experience.
  - o Where are the operational jobs? Who is taking those jobs and why? What barriers keep women from taking and succeeding in those jobs? What support from HR, senior leadership, a person who had that role in the past, and peers can be offered to ensure success in a risky job?
- *Exposure* – Leaders need to see the women more frequently in order to know them and to know how they think. Organizations can actively facilitate the development of relationships by tracking across organizational opportunities, by seeking ways to ensure that the talented women are widely known, and by using mentors to develop breadth.
  - o Are women widely known? How much exposure do they have across the organization? Do

leaders know how they think and what they can do?

- *Behavioral Norms* – Not following the accepted norms of behavior within the organization or not being "like" others in leadership positions is a tricky process. Organizations need to be honest about styles – what is acceptable and what is not – and they need to be tolerant of a different approach that does deliver results.
- *Strategic Outlook* – Organizations are increasingly saying that women are not "strategic enough" in addition to the usual adages of not being tough enough or being too tough.
  - What does it mean in your organization to be strategic? How do leaders demonstrate strategic capability? Do women have the appropriate opportunity?

Recommendations for Women

Women can take action on their own behalf:

- **Recognize that performance is only one criterion by which a person is judged.** Peer support, connections that will help get things done through others, self-confidence in the ability to lead, and a host of other factors matter as well.

- **Relationships are an important asset that need to be built and nurtured.** Make time to talk with people on issues that are not immediate to the current task, particularly during times of chaos and change. Bosses, peers, subordinates and others across the organization need to feel that they know their colleagues in order to have a sense of their capability.

- **Find common ground.** Since relationships matter so much, business cannot just be all about "business." Often it is the tangential elements such as ideas, hobbies, interests or passions that help forge the bonds between people.

- **Credibility is vital.** Credibility comes in part from what has been done in the past, the importance of the accomplishments to the organization, the degree to which those accomplishments are known, and the people with whom one is connected.

- **To advance, one has to be judged as "strategic."** Figure out what that definition means. Strive to support that definition and gain requisite experience.

- **Confidence and presence matter enormously – cultivate both.** One trait begets the other.

- **Perfectionism can be both an asset and a liability.** Recognize the downsides of each behavior, and make a conscious choice about what is truly needed in a given situation. Sometimes an 80% solution is the better option.

- **The most successful leaders admit their mistakes, find a solution and move on.** Dwelling on what went wrong impedes progress.

- **Practice being patient.** Patience can convey confidence and a sense of control to which others respond favorably.

- **Feedback is essential to developing and honing skills.** Seek information from others on a specific situation that was observed so that the input is accurate and the perspective is valid. Then decide what to do with the opinion – accept it, reject it, change behaviors or do nothing.

- **Mentors, godfathers and advocates are critical.** Going it alone can be an insurmountable task. Having the right person share knowledge, advice, insight and nuances is invaluable. Without such mentoring, it is easy to fall off the radar screen when key positions are being filled. It is also hard to learn how to influence the organization without senior guidance on how the organization works.

- **Working for just one boss can be disadvantageous to career progression.** If the boss leaves, retires, or falls out of favor, then there is no champion and scant support. Working for different people is often essential to advancement.

- **Find time for informal conversations with colleagues during times of strategic change.** Share information and ideas, talk about eagerness for new responsibilities and interests. To discuss such matters at scheduled meetings that have a more rigid agenda may not be as effective.

- **Recognition or praise rarely occurs at senior levels.** Instead, a lack of criticism may be the only recognition for a job well done, so find ways to talk about accomplishments that do not appear disingenuous or overly self-promoting.

- **Proactively seek opportunities.** Opportunities are earned, given and taken. Take calculated risks – and deliver.

- **Trust your own judgment.** If a conclusion has been reached, stand by it. Self-doubt is counter-productive.

- **Familiarity matters.** Organizations derive comfort from predictability in their leaders so they know what to expect as the leaders move into new roles.

- **Changing the organization from the outside is virtually impossible.** Effective change comes from the inside, which means learning the rules of engagement and playing to areas of strength.

Recommendations for Organizations

Talented women are in short supply in almost every organization. For women to reach their full potential, it behooves the organization to be aware of the obstacles that might stand in their way. The following recommendations should minimize the chances of losing top performers.

- **Map developmental assignments for high-potential women that the organization wants to retain.** Note the developmental jobs and how long women are in those positions (if ever), the support necessary for their success, and whether or not assumptions about them have been made accurately.

- **Create pathways for operational experience.** Quite often, women do not get sufficient operational experience, which is critical at senior levels regardless of the position or the function. Where are the operational jobs, who is taking those jobs and why, what barriers keep women from taking and succeeding in those jobs? What mechanisms need to be in place for a woman to succeed in a risky job?

- **Provide constructive feedback.** Make sure that advancing women have a clear, concise picture of how the organization sees them, their leadership, and their capabilities. Ensure they know what behaviors to change or adapt.

- **Arrange on-going support through godfathering, mentoring and advocacy.** Designate senior leaders who can provide advice, insight and experiential knowledge to shorten the learning curve. Ensure that women understand the positive, constructive implications of the help that is being offered, as opposed to viewing the advice as criticism or a judgment that they are incompetent.

- **Increase transparency in talent discussions.** In discussions about performance, encourage those providing the critique to specify what qualities such as "being strategic, tough or ready" really mean.

- **Train and develop.** Give women the tools and capabilities to engage the organization in the best possible way. Help bosses understand how to be inclusive and to develop talent that is not a mirror-image of themselves.

- **Encourage an inclusive culture.** Often the best ideas and solutions come when a diverse range of voices are involved and included. Develop the organizational capability to adapt to different styles.

- **Actively facilitate a process of exposure and recognition.** Learn and observe how women think and act in a broad cross-section of circumstances.

- **Focus on developing a strategic perspective.** Organizations are increasingly saying that women are not "strategic enough" in addition to the usual adages of not being tough enough or being too tough. What does it mean to be strategic? How do leaders demonstrate strategic capability? Do women have the appropriate chances for such opportunities?

- **Honestly assess behavioral and cultural norms.** What is or is not acceptable, and under what circumstances and to what degree of tolerance?

Recommendations for Bosses

- **Offer direct, honest, timely feedback that is positive, negative and most of all, constructive.** Make sure women understand what has been communicated; how the advice works for a woman and that they know what to do differently.

- **Be inclusive.** Think about the actions that ensure everyone on the team is heard, is correctly acknowledged, and is included in critical discussions.

- **Increase exposure.** Advocate project and task force assignments for women that build exposure across the organization.

- **Examine behavioral norms.** Question whether or not style is an issue and if it needs to be adjusted. Be honest about the truly critical components for success and the reasons why they are critical.

- **Evaluate operational assignments.** When a woman takes an operational role, ensure that she is positioned to succeed and that she gets the required support and resources from her team and her peers.
- **Manage the isolation.** Track whether talented women are becoming isolated and appropriately intervene where possible.

APPENDIX A

Interview Topics for Women

Below is a list of topics we would like to explore with you in the interview.

The challenge of being the first or the only woman

Most women in senior positions today have been the first women to occupy a particular position throughout many of their promotions. If they are not the first, then they are frequently the only. Being unique in any culture can accentuate style differences, create a sense of isolation, and limit ability to access the network.

We want to hear about issues such as the following:

- Your experiences in being the first or the only woman to the extent that this applies to you
- The ways you learned to manage that situation
- The results for you personally (both positively and negatively)

In addition, we want to hear about the challenges of (or lack of)

- Matching your style with that of the corporation where style – this can include among other things issues such as collaborative approach, comfort with hierarchy vs. team, inclusivity, building consensus and commitment, expectations about how success is acknowledged, and expected recognition
- Having your voice heard in a male dominated culture
- Being visible to the rest of the organization – e.g., other women wanting to see a woman in the c-suite, increased demands of being the only woman, being watched, mentoring expectations, etc.
- Any other experiences related to style

Making the transition to senior leadership

All leaders are challenged by the transition from being a significant manager to being a senior leader. We are interested in your perspective on the following leadership transitions:

- Coping with areas of grey and with taking risks
- Internal support mechanisms (e.g., peers, bosses, mentors, coaches) in making the transition – help in learning the job, help in recognizing barriers, preparation for the role
- Loneliness
- Competitiveness among peers
- Being authentic
- Fun in the job

- Sense of having contributed enough
- Being tired of the game
- Managing inevitable conflicts
- Managing power – signaling positions of power, coping with the impact of power plays, thinking several moves ahead of current power struggles (e.g., chess game mentality), staffing patterns

Perceptions
- The ways in which people perceive you in the organization... how they would describe you ... the gender roles in which individuals place you -- e.g., as wives or mothers, particularly in struggles for authority and power

Living within the acceptable norms of the corporation
All corporate cultures have an accepted band of behavior which includes what is and what is not tolerated within the corporations – e.g., rage, outbursts, confrontation, or failure. For men as well as for women, behaviors outside the accepted gender norms can also be a challenge. We want to hear about your experiences in the following:

- Restraining emotional reactions and personal style to fit within perceived acceptable range – the energy required, the emotional toll, and the misattributions from peers
- Showing emotion such as rage and hurt

- Admitting mistakes
- Whistle blowing
- The nature of relationships with peers -- e.g., the shallow qualities of relationships, the variation between being idealized on one hand and being a scapegoat on the other, the opportunities for social interaction and networking
- The culture of the organization and ways it impacts you
- Activities that are/are not part of the corporate norm -- don't play golf – not unacceptable but you do not participate
- The mediating effects of a congenial vs. uncongenial environment, or of an inclusive culture

Promotions and Career Development

Early in careers, talented women appear to be promoted quickly based on merit. We want to know about your career progression, your career moves, and the advancement of your career in the following:

- The cycle of promotions – e.g., speed of being promoted to the next level, being promoted a couple of levels ahead to serve diversity agendas, not being promoted, waiting to ensure the person is fully prepared for the next level, and such
- The opportunities provided for development – e.g., the types of opportunities women usually get and don't

get such as fix-its, start-ups, turnarounds, changes in scale and scope

- Opportunities that broaden the experience base

Life-stage issues

- What events have raised questions about the choices regarding work and why?
- Are life choices, consciously or unconsciously, a significant detriment to a woman's career or not – in what ways have your personal choices affected your career?
- Opinions about life-choices and how those affect career choices?

Relationships

At senior levels, the quality of the peer-to-peer relationships appears to matter more than many other variables in enabling a leader to accomplish goals and implement strategy. What have been your experiences with the quality of your peer-to-peer relationships? Boss? Board? Direct reports?

Competitive Positions

At the senior levels, competition for the next advancement increases as does competition for resources, time with the CEO, one stance versus another, and so forth. We are interested in your perspective on competition with your male colleagues and with your female colleagues. How competitive do you see yourself being with colleagues?

Procedure for Interview

In the list above are the topics we want to explore and the interview will largely follow these topics. However, we will not structure this as a formal series of questions but will pursue more of an exploration and discussion about your own experiences and perceptions.

APPENDIX B

Interview Topics for Men

Introduction

- I want to hear your point of view – I am not asking you to represent all men.
- I am not asking you to generalize for all women – rather think about the senior women you have worked with, describe your experience of working with them, and I will generalize across the interviews.
- I will not ask about any specific women – but feel free to use stories to illustrate your points – feel free to give an example of one person if you choose.
- I want to hear your observations and advice
- The information is confidential – I will not disclose anything that identifies you or your company

Topics

1. What do you think are the biggest challenges for women as senior leaders?
2. Over the last five to ten years, in general, what have you seen women at senior levels do that increases their effectiveness as leaders? What have you seen

women do that decreases their effectiveness as leaders?

3. In thinking about your female colleagues, what do you observe about how they manage the following relationships (both positively and negatively):

    a. With their teams?

    b. With their bosses and boss' boss?

    c. With their peers?

4. We often hear someone within the organization say that a woman is either "not tough enough" or "too tough," particularly in discussions about promotion. In your experience, what do women do (and not do) that leads you to evaluate them as too tough? As not tough enough?

5. What would you like your female colleagues to do more of? To do differently?

6. Describe the characteristics of a woman that you would be willing to work for at this point in your career.

7. If you could offer any advice to women (whether it is politically correct or incorrect) on how to reach the top jobs in the company, what would you say?

Two questions about you as a leader:

1. Describe the nature of your relationships with each of the following.

   a. Your team.

   b. Your boss and your boss' boss.

   c. Your peers.

2. As one rises in the corporate hierarchy, competition with peers in the "tournament" for the next job is inevitable. How do you approach this internal competition – what's your style, how do you think about competing, what is your frame of reference?

APPENDIX C

Sponsoring Companies

AstraZeneca

British Telecom

Cardinal Health

Deutsche Bank

FleetBoston Financial (now Bank of America)

International Truck and Engine

Kellogg

Motorola

PricewaterhouseCoopers

Siemens Financial

Wanda T. Wallace, Ph.D.

Dr. Wanda Wallace is President and CEO of Leadership Forum, Inc. LFI designs and delivers innovative programs that enable leaders to improve not only their leadership ability, but also their skills in strategic thought, team building, talent development, cultural inclusivity and strategic execution. As a consultant and educator who is equally at ease in the distinct worlds of business and education, she has designed a number of highly rated programs that have been enthusiastically received on both sides of the Atlantic. Dr. Wallace has forged close relationships with a number of blue-chip clients, including ABB, Allianz Group, British Petroleum, British Telecom, Citigroup, Deutsche Bank, Ericsson, DaimlerChrysler, Ford Motor Company, Goldman Sachs, GlaxoSmithKline,

International Truck and Engine, ITT, LG, Merrill Lynch, Philips, PricewaterhouseCoopers and Unilever.

Prior to founding Leadership Forum, Inc., she was Executive Vice President of Duke Corporate Education, Inc., which she joined after her tenure as Associate Dean of Executive Education and professor of marketing at The Fuqua School of Business at Duke University.

Dr. Wallace received her Ph.D. from the Psychology Department at Duke University with special emphasis on cognitive and thought processes. In addition to teaching at Duke, Dr. Wallace has also taught at the Kenan-Flagler Business School at the University of North Carolina at Chapel Hill.

She frequently speaks at large scale events as well as company-specific functions, and also teaches short and multi-day seminars and coaches senior executive women.

CPSIA information can be obtained at www.ICGtesting.com
Printed in the USA
BVOW07s1812180713

326192BV00003B/978/P